MORE ADVANCE PRAISE FOR THE NEW MURPHY'S LAW

"For those of you who have enjoyed Emmett's writing in *Leadership IQ* and *The Genius of Sitting Bull*, it will be no surprise that *The New Murphy's Law* is a book that is value-based, growth-producing, and fun. Reading any of Emmett's work is a treat. Emmett managed to take real people in real life situations and tell their stories in a way that is inspirational and instructive. While reading about these real people, the reader is informed about the values demonstrated in the lives of these people and lessons we can all learn. Perhaps the most poignant part of the book is Emmett's reflection regarding his father's values and what he learned from these values. Beautifully done."

— Irwin Hansen, Chief Executive Officer,
Summit Health System

"*The New Murphy's Law* is a very inspiring book, and not just for businesspeople; it's a wonderful guide for meeting the challenges and seizing the opportunities of everyday life. I think every parent should read the book, then use it to teach their children well."

—Steve Bennett, author of *The Plugged-In Parent: What Everyone Must Know About Kids, Computers, and Technology*

"*The New Murphy's Law* unlocks the power of optimism—the healing and connecting energy we need to quell the anxiety of an uncertain world. The 10 rules are a road map to life's journey—for each fork in the road, there's a rule to help you continue on—in the right direction, of course!"

— Lillee Gelinas, Vice President, Clinical Improvement and Chief Nursing Officer,
Volunteer Hospital Association of America Inc.

"A remarkable book. *The New Murphy's Law* inspires us to fulfill our dreams and help others."

— Norma Carr-Ruffino, Ph.D.,
author of *The Promotable Woman*

"Everyday wisdom, courage and responsibility that provides us a blueprint to attain a richer and more optimistic life. Simple, elegant and inspirational rules to live by."

— Leo Lopez, Chairman and CEO,
Eligibility Services, Inc.

"I've known Dr. Murphy for several years, as both a professional mentor and a personal friend. The delightful thing about this work is that one can see a little bit of him in every chapter. *The New Murphy's Law* portrays ordinary people, doing extraordinary things. In this treasure chest of stories Emmett reminds us that by embracing life's challenges, we not only improve our own lives, but the world around us. This is the kind of book you want to read, then place on your bedstand for constant reference and reassurance. When everyday stress starts to get the upper hand, just reread a few chapters and you too can be a "pragmatic optimist." Thank you Dr. Murphy for sharing your family's legacy."

— Linda McKnight Buchanan,
Service Line Leader, Kaiser Permanente

"Incredibly uplifting! In a world of 'can't,', this book says you 'can' and then artfully shows you how."
— Hap Klopp, author of *The Adventure of Leadership* and *The Complete Idiot's Guide to Business Management*

"A book designed to give ordinary souls the courage and spirit to achieve extraordinary feats. The messages and stories of *The New Murphy's Law* remind each of us that we can make a difference in this world and in our daily work."

> — Marilyn Chow, R.N., Ph.D., Former President
> and CEO, National League for Healthcare;
> National Advisory Council, U.S. Department of
> Health and Human Services

"On the heels of *Leadership IQ* comes some great new advice from Emmett Murphy. *The New Murphy's Law* dispenses some practical advice and inspiring insight for the 21st century that is applicable today."

> — Ingo Zinner, Director of Human Resources,
> Hewlett-Packard

"Wonderful, lively storytelling. I read this book with real pleasure and loved learning the lessons of success from real people, many of whom I thought I knew much better than I did."

> — Pamela Gilberd, author of *The Eleven
> Commandments of Wildly Successful Women*

The New Murphy's Law

The New Murphy's Law

10 Unconventional Rules for Making Everything Go Right in Your Life and Work

EMMETT C. MURPHY

Chandler House Press
Worcester, Massachusetts
1998

Published by

Chandler House Press

335 Chandler Street
Worcester, MA 01602
USA

President: Lawrence J. Abramoff
Publisher/Editor-in-Chief: Richard J. Staron
Vice President of Sales: Irene S. Bergman
Editorial/Production Manager: Jennifer J. Goguen
Book Design: Bookmakers
Cover Design: Emily Weadock

Chandler House Press books are available at special discounts for bulk purchases. For more information about how to arrange such purchases, please contact Irene Bergman at Chandler House Press, 335 Chandler Street, Worcester, MA 01602, or call (800) 642-6657, or fax (508) 756-9425, or find us on the World Wide Web at www.tatnuck.com.

Chandler House Press books are distributed to the trade by

National Book Network, Inc.
4720 Boston Way
Lanham, MD 20706
(800) 462-6420

To Emmett Sr.

and

Carol

Contents

Acknowledgments

The genesis for this book was my father, Emmett Sr., whose life and teachings continue to influence my life as I progress through the stages he handled with such grace and good humor. The inspiration to write it came from my wife and life partner, Carol, who continually draws me back to the lessons it teaches. I dedicate it to them both with love and respect.

The book itself could not have come into existence without the help of a team that came to believe as much in its message as I did. I owe each of them a special note of gratitude. My agent, friend and collaborator, Michael Snell, helped me understand that *The New Murphy's Law* is about "showing the way," not "telling the way," and applied his wonderful creative talents to help me bring it to life. Dick Staron, our publisher and friend at Chandler House, encouraged me to speak to the universal search for hope that lies within each of us. And, a team of associates at E.C. Murphy, Ltd. helped me research and interpret the data, lessons and life stories that translate *The New Murphy's Law* into action. They include Kimberly Leanos, who served as overall copy editor, Amy Penasack, William Paterson and Sharon DeJoy, who researched and developed key concepts.

And, finally, I want to thank our Murphy family team for encouraging the effort throughout: my late mother, Florence, who taught us all how to "run toward the lion's roar," my brothers and sisters—Patrick, Virginia, Glen and Ann—who live the axiom "don't just communicate, connect," and my children, Mark Andrew, my intellectual partner, who helped me organize and mine the research, and Marissa Eileen, my personal ethicist, who kept me grounded in the values that framed the whole effort.

Connections

Please, "don't just communicate, connect": share your ideas and questions with us by:

- ♣ calling (716) 759-2491
- ♣ faxing (716) 759-1320
- ♣ e-mailing www.newmurphyslaw.com

Introduction: The New Murphy's Law

"If anything should go right, you can make it go right."

Emmett C. Murphy Sr.

♣ MR. FANTASTIC

My father gave me a priceless gift. Realizing that for him the end was near, and having lived a full life, he looked up at me from his bed when I asked, "How are you doing, Dad?" smiled, and said, "I'm fantastic, son!" It was a standing joke between us, but it epitomized my father's beliefs and attitude toward life. And death. I treasure that gift.

Not long after that, he passed away peacefully. As for myself, like most children whose parents have lived a full life and harvested value from the joys and sorrows along the way, I paused to reflect on my inheritance.

THE NEW MURPHY'S LAW

No, I didn't inherit a lot of money or other material assets. My father, Emmett C. Murphy Sr., was not a wealthy man. But I did inherit a belief, a set of values and a guiding principle for life that have served me better than any trust fund ever could. It's what I like to call *The New Murphy's Law*.

I grew up in upstate New York, where the snow doesn't just fall from the sky, it avalanches down, burying the lawn, the driveway and the sidewalk with what seemed to me as a child like insurmountable, unmovable mountains of the white stuff. I remember my father breaking shovels as he struggled to clear a path for the mailman, Mr. Ferry, who adhered to the old maxim that the mail will go through no matter what. The two men would meet on the sidewalk—Mr. Ferry bundled up from head to toe, my father sweating from his exertions and stripped down to a sweatshirt. "A gorgeous day, Mr. Ferry," my father would say, to which the mailman would respond, "'Tis that, Mr. Murphy. And how are you doing this fine day?" My father would grin, raise his shovel in salute and respond, "I am *fantastic*, Mr. Ferry!" That brought a chuckle from Mr. Ferry, "Top of the mornin' to you, Mr. Fantastic."

Mr. Fantastic. That nickname became part of neighborhood lore, and it caused no small measure of consternation for a young boy on the threshold of adolescent rebellion. One day I confronted my father with my opinion that it was foolish to say life is always fantastic. "Mr. O'Connell lost his job, the Devlins are getting a divorce, Tommy Callahan had to have heart surgery," I pointed out. "Things go wrong all the time, but you just keep saying everything's fantastic. I don't understand."

I can't recall whether Murphy Sr. sighed, frowned, smiled or laughed, but I can still see him sitting me down at the kitchen table and delivering a short speech that would forever change the way I looked at the world.

"There are two kinds of Murphys," he said. "There's the Old Murphy, and there's the New Murphy. I may be your old man, but I'm a New Murphy, and you're an Old Murphy."

I had no idea what he was talking about until he elaborated. "Look, son, most people agree with the Old Murphy's Law, that if anything can go wrong, it will go wrong. I happen to believe in the New Murphy's Law, that if anything should go right, I can *make* it go right. I choose hope, rather than despair, to guide my life. The Old Murphy's Law provides an excuse for failure, the New Murphy's Law gives you faith in success."

If anything should go right, I can make it go right. Over the years I have kept that motto in my heart, and it has served me well. I have enjoyed the support of a close-knit and loving family, I have had good fortune in my career and business, and I have been granted the privilege of working with other people to create success through my consultation and writing. It doesn't just work for me, either. Through my travels and research over the past thirty-plus years, I have met and worked with thousands of other believers in the New Murphy's Law. By studying the way they live their lives and do their work I have discovered ten rules that anyone can follow to translate the New Murphy's Law into action and achieve ever-greater personal and professional success.

That's what this book is about. In the pages ahead you will meet some remarkable people who have replaced despair with hope, failure with success, "I'm okay" with "I'm fantastic." Like *The New Murphy's Law* itself, these rules often turn conventional wisdom upside down.

❧ PRAGMATIC OPTIMISM

Before we explore these ten rules, however, I'd like to pause here for a moment to talk about what I call *pragmatic optimism*. Murphy Sr. was a pragmatic optimist.

As I progressed through my own development, discussing and sometimes complaining about my problems, my father would remind me that the opportunity to face such challenges was reason enough for hope. As my mother, Florence Sullivan Murphy, said, my father saw the everyday process of life, and the challenges that come with it, as reason for celebration. He knew that hope must not remain an abstract concept, but must be tested and strengthened by facing the everyday problems of career and personal life. He viewed hope as the product of responsibility and knew, as the philosopher George Santayana observed, that "words without action are the assassins of idealism."

Pragmatic optimists are grateful to be alive and couple hope with action, steadfastly believing that people can always create better results in their lives. Where Old Murphys blame fate for failure and flee from personal responsibility, New Murphys take responsibility for failure, as well as success, and the opportunity it offers to learn how to take better control of their lives. They realize that optimism is like a muscle that is strengthened through the practical exercise of everyday problem solving.

This concept of pragmatic optimism is the unifying principle for the ten rules that translate the New Murphy's Law into action. These rules would have pleased my father, for they provide a blueprint by which anyone mired in the pessimism of the Old Murphy's Law can build a life of hope.

♣ Rule 1: Run Toward the Roar

♣ Rule 2: Don't Just Communicate, Connect

♣ Rule 3: Make Change Your Constant Ally

♣ Rule 4: Gain Power by Giving It Away

♣ Rule 5: Practice Strategic Humility

♣ Rule 6: Put Your Time Where It Really Counts

♣ Rule 7: Throw Anger Away

♣ Rule 8: Do the Right Thing

♣ Rule 9: Give More Than You Receive

♣ Rule 10: Never, Never, Never Give Up

Each chapter in this book will explore one of these ten rules for success and show how real people practice them. Our examples come from every walk of life and from the vast treasury of our collective human experience, and these stories provide parables from which we can learn valuable lessons about the power of pragmatic optimism that resides in us all.

♣ THE WIZARD WITHIN

L. Frank Baum's novel *The Wizard of Oz* and the film based on the book have enchanted millions of people around the world, in no small part because the story teaches a timeless lesson. Dorothy and her companions—the lion, the scarecrow and the tin woodsman—followed the yellow brick road to the Emerald City because they thought a powerful wizard could fulfill their dreams to get back to Kansas, gain courage, obtain a brain, and develop a heart. In the end, of course, they discovered that they had possessed the means to accomplish their goals all along. No wizard could solve their problems, only they themselves could do so after a long and perilous journey of self-discovery.

Whatever your own goals and desires, you'll realize them if you continue your journey with hope, pragmatic optimism, and faith in the New Murphy's Law. In the pages ahead we will travel deeply into the rules that translate the New Murphy's Law into action, meeting people who demonstrate the power of those rules along the way.

If you see a chapter that seems to speak directly to your own life or work situation, feel free to go right to that chapter, skipping the preceding ones. I've designed the book for easy, random access, although you may also read it from cover to cover.

Before you read further, I invite you to pause for a few minutes and reflect on your own yellow brick road. Think about where you've been, where you are now, the destination you want to reach five or ten years from now. That arc of your life, that rainbow of possibilities, does not just unfold at random: it flows from the beliefs and values that guide your life and shape every decision you make about how to live it. Expect the worst, and it will happen. Expect the best, as my father always did, and you will get it. Believe this: "If anything can go right, I can *make* it go right."

Rule 1

Run Toward the Roar

"Courage is being scared to death...
and saddling up anyway."

John Wayne

♣ COURAGE UNDER FIRE

Imagine that you're an antelope grazing in a clearing when a lion's roar suddenly splits the air. Would your natural instinct propel you to flee in the opposite direction? If so, you would be running toward almost certain death, because lions expect their prey to do just that. The male of the pride moves stealthily to the precise position the antelope would logically select as its best escape route, while the lionesses lie in ambush directly opposite the male. With the trap in place, the lion roars with all his might. The startled antelope, of course, runs away from the roar—and into the jaws of the waiting lionesses.

When faced with threats to our happiness or security, we humans all too often run away from the "roar" of daily life only to find ourselves encountering a situation far more treacherous than the one we thought we were fleeing. We, like the antelope, must come to realize that survival and success lie in the direction of the roaring lion.

This lesson applies to the everyday world of work and personal life. Upon close examination, an event that seems quite threatening on the surface, such as a conflict with your boss, often turns out to pose far less danger than other circumstances, such as losing your job or failing to perform to your highest potential. Rather than flee the conflict, you should concentrate on solving the problem. In other words, when something goes wrong in your life, run toward—not away from—the roar.

Marliese Mitchell, one of the most interesting clients and friends I've ever had, followed this rule throughout her life. Immigrating to the United States from Germany as a young woman, Mitchell supported herself by working as a leg model for advertisers—a job she saw as a stop-gap until she could settle on the right career. Toward that end, she used her earnings to put herself through college, where she discovered her life's work: nursing.

After graduation, Mitchell did indeed become a nurse but, before long, she grew restless and decided that she wanted to tackle an even greater challenge: to earn a Master's degree and pursue a career in hospital administration. A mother of five at this point, the courageous nurse began her graduate work at Harvard University without ever shirking her responsibilities at home.

After Mitchell earned her MBA, she rapidly advanced up the professional ladder from staff nurse to president of the world's largest international hospital consulting firm. That's when she heard the roar. During her first assignment at a Southeast Asian hospital, she uncovered a potential scandal involving the sale of baby boys. Her colleagues advised her not to get involved in an investigation of this rumored scandal; if her suspicions proved wrong, they warned her, probing into the issue could ruin her career. But Mitchell could not turn her back on the roar. What if the rumors and vague accusations were true? She knew that she could not live with herself if she ignored them.

Instead of putting on blinders and quietly backing away, Mitchell chose to plunge headlong into a search for the truth. She assigned herself to the hospital as a staff nurse, working incognito with people in the front line of service. Within just three weeks, Marliese Mitchell discovered a situation far more horrific than she could have imagined. A criminal network of caregivers, physicians and high-level government officials were conspiring to purchase baby girls on the slave market, surgically change them into males, then resell them for adoption at a higher rate.

Almost single-handedly, Mitchell uncovered evidence that led to criminal convictions of the conspirators—an effort that caught the attention and support of the United Nations, the World Health Organization, the United States, and other governments. Though she hadn't set out to do so, Mitchell ended up winning a reputation as one of the most capable and tenacious healthcare leaders in the world. By running toward, rather than away from, the roar, she had made something very wrong go right.

Marliese Mitchell's story underscores the tremendous impact of one person's courageous actions. Who knows how many hundreds, or even thousands, of innocent baby girls may have been mutilated and then sold if Marliese had not chosen bravery over complacency? Courage, bravery, the resolve to set things right no matter how high the personal risk—these traits separate the Old Murphys from the New Murphys. We all possess the potential for bravery in the midst of peril, though some of us must reach deep within ourselves to find it. In this chapter, we will examine four reasons that should motivate each of us to run toward the roar.

FOUR REASONS FOR BRAVERY

1 Do It for Yourself
2 Do It for Your Team
3 Do It for Your Community
4 Do It for the World

Although courage takes many different forms, it begins with a dedication to make something go right even when doing so seems to pose an immediate threat. That immediate threat pales in light of the long-term danger created by doing nothing.

Have you ever hoped to achieve a personal or professional goal only to have others express their doubts about your ability to reach it? If friends, family, or coworkers doubt you, do you muster the courage to stand alone and insist upon your own capabilities?

Do you consider yourself a "team player"? If you see the welfare, or even the lives, of other members of your team in jeopardy, can you step forward and fight for their well-being?

Have you ever recognized an injustice or inequity in the community? If so, did you quietly carp about its unfairness or did you stand up for your beliefs against the status quo?

If a courageous sacrifice on your part could benefit all of posterity, would you act boldly and set your own fears aside?

The stories that follow will show how you can run toward the roar in your own life and work.

🍀 DO IT FOR YOURSELF

Today, John Hockenberry enjoys enviable success in his career, working as a reporter for the popular television news magazine show, *Dateline NBC*, and as host of his own weekly program on MSNBC, the network's burgeoning cable enterprise. Not so long ago, however, Hockenberry's future did not look so bright.

In 1976, while still a student at the University of Chicago, Hockenberry and his college roommate decided to hitchhike to Massachusetts over spring break. In Pennsylvania they got a ride with two female college students who, it turned out, had been driving for a solid twelve hours with no rest. In the middle of the afternoon on that clear, sunny day, Hockenberry and the other occupants of the Chevy Nova, including the driver, drifted off to sleep. They were awakened violently and suddenly when the Chevy burst through a guardrail at the edge of Interstate 80 in Pennsylvania, then rolled pell-mell down the embankment.

Amazingly, Hockenberry remained alert throughout the entire accident, even as the car rolled over four times, with the frame crashing repeatedly into his back. As he reflects in his recent memoir, *Moving Violations: War Zones, Wheelchairs, and Declarations of Independence* (Hyperion, 1995), "I made a solitary attempt to leave the car, placing my hands on my knees in an effort to push off and straighten up.... Upon touching those knees and feeling the sensation only in my hands, I knew. My spinal cord had been severed. Whatever else was wrong with me, I would not walk again. The most powerful sensation I have ever felt is of no sensation at all."

Of the four occupants of the Chevy Nova, only the driver died. Hockenberry's roommate and the driver's friend both escaped from the ordeal virtually unscathed. Hockenberry, however, suffered a fractured skull, along with a broken shoulder, collarbone and ribs. All of these injuries, though, meant little compared to the injury inflicted on his back that day; the broken bones would heal, but not the spinal cord. Paralyzed from the chest down, Hockenberry soon knew that he would live the rest of his life in a wheelchair.

Hockenberry spent the better part of a year recuperating from his injuries and participating in a rehabilitation program near his parents' home in Michigan. He found the rehabilitation process difficult and grueling, but not nearly as challenging as the psychological recovery. Yet, while feelings of fear and helplessness swept through his mind, Hockenberry did not allow himself to wallow in self-pity. Instead, he let go of all unproductive emotions and resolved to put his life back together. Only one year after the accident, he began to regain his "normal" life, returning to the University of Chicago to resume his studies.

Given his dedication to recovery, he would not let anything get in his way, not even the university's limited wheelchair access to only one building on campus. When high snowdrifts built up during the winter, Hockenberry could scarcely maneuver around campus, let alone into classrooms. With the university unwilling or unable to remedy the situation, Hockenberry gave up on the school, but he never gave up on himself.

Listening to a distant roar urging him toward success, he eventually transferred to the University of Oregon, where he lived by himself in a small apartment and found a job as an employment trainer in a nursing home for developmentally disabled adults. Here, he would face a new series of challenges.

When his supervisor at the nursing home openly doubted his ability to do the job because of his confinement to a wheelchair, Hockenberry decided to prove her wrong. As he writes in his memoir, he vowed to "work like a maniac," responding to her qualms "with the obsessive energy of a combat general." He did not disappoint himself, or his supervisor. As he explains, "Before I was hired at the care center, the second shift had been far behind in its programs and paperwork. A week after I was on the job, we were far ahead of schedule."

When a career in journalism beckoned him, Hockenberry approached that goal with the same fervor and confidence he had exhibited at the care center. In 1980, he approached the local public radio station in Eugene, KLCC, volunteering his services as a reporter. That job provided his first major professional break when, in May of that year, Mount Saint Helens, a long-dormant volcano, violently erupted. Since station KLCC was situated closest to the eruption, it became the primary source of news coverage on the disaster for National Public Radio (NPR). Initially Howard Berkes, the station's top reporter, covered the story exclusively, leaving Hockenberry to deal with all the other news in the area. Eventually, when Berkes moved on to become a regular network correspondent, NPR editors in Washington, DC gave Hockenberry the prime Mount Saint Helens assignment.

Since that time, Hockenberry's disability has not prevented him from progressing rapidly in his career or from tackling the toughest assignments. For example, after lobbying his editors and assuring them he could get the story, Hockenberry traveled to the Gaza strip to cover the 1987 Palestinian uprising, a tough assignment even for an able-bodied reporter.

Happily, the reporter's wheelchair proved less an impediment than either he or his editors had feared.

Even in the toughest circumstances or the most tense situations, people consistently offered their help by pushing his chair or even, at times, by carrying him on their shoulders. His remarkable bravery always inspired admiration, never pity.

In the years since, Hockenberry has dedicated much of his time and effort to advance more than his own career, working to make sure that all disabled people receive the opportunity and the means to remove the obstacles that stand between them and their goals. He has written and lectured extensively on the need to protect and strictly enforce laws that benefit the disabled. As he explains, "For the struggle I've gone through to mean something, I have to be an activist." Having worked so arduously to chip away at the stereotypes and preconceptions that threatened to deter him from achieving his own goals, John Hockenberry has shown the way for others to run toward the roar.

🍀 Do It for Your Team

The roar that Audie Murphy heard was one that resounded throughout the entire world: World War II. Murphy, an actor who achieved considerable Hollywood fame in the 1950s, won worldwide acclaim before he even set foot in front of a camera—for numerous displays of real-life courage that a screenwriter could scarcely dream up.

As a young soldier on the battlefields of World War II, Audie Murphy faced life-threatening situations every day without the luxury of a director behind him to shout "cut" when the going got rough. He fought bravely—to save his fellow soldiers' skins as well as his own—and became the most decorated American soldier of World War II. His sense of responsibility to his fellow soldiers and his country led him to risk his own life on dozens of occasions, many chronicled in the movie based on his life, *To Hell and Back*.

The first of Murphy's countless courageous acts took place on August 15, 1944, not long after he arrived on French soil. He and a friend, Private Lattie Tipton, were assigned to hold their position on an enemy-fortified hill. Following that order with a vengeance, Murphy threw himself into the fray, slaying two enemies before turning his attention to a labyrinth of nearby foxholes. After running out of ammunition, he traversed a barrage of German bullets and soldiers to seize a weapon from the body of a fallen enemy. He then ascended the hill once more and finished off the men in the foxholes. With his good friend Private Tipton at his side, Murphy had succeeded in his mission.

One man, outnumbered ten-to-one, had left the enemy reeling. As the smoke cleared and the dust settled, Private Tipton stepped forward to accept an offer of surrender from the surviving Germans, only to find himself victim of a ruse when a burst of gunfire cut him down. Murphy would later say of that moment: "I remember the experience as I do a nightmare. A demon seems to have entered my body." Still badly outnumbered, he could rely on no one but himself. Refusing to give up, he killed two more enemies with a grenade and then concentrated on the machine gun crew who had killed Tipton. With his adrenaline flowing, Murphy raced toward the enemy stronghold and destroyed every last member of the opposition. "His extraordinary heroism resulted in the capture of a fiercely contested enemy-held hill and the capture of the entire enemy garrison," read the dedication on the Distinguished Service Cross he won for his efforts that day.

For most people, these acts of singular courage might have been enough for a lifetime. But Audie Murphy continued hearing the roar—and running toward it. Just a few months later, in another instance of uncommon valor, he found himself pitted alone against an oncoming charge of German troops. The only obstacle between the approaching enemy and the U.S. 15th Infantry, Murphy instinctively held his ground. At a moment like this, fear can impel an individual to an impulsive act of self-preservation; but instead of retreating to safety, Audie Murphy once again chose to fight.

Jumping onto a burning tank, he single-handedly fought off six other tanks and two rifle companies. By turning back the enemy, he probably saved the lives of thousands of American soldiers who would have perished in the planned attack. In addition, he preserved the American position, not allowing it to be overrun as it surely would have had he not acted so courageously. Rather than save his own life, he risked it to protect his fellow soldiers and his country.

Murphy's courage in the heat of battle became almost routine as he miraculously survived engagement after engagement throughout World War II, committing one act of bravery after another. All told, he single-handedly eliminated more than 200 enemy soldiers during his tour of duty. Widely regarded as the nation's greatest soldier ever, Murphy continually ran toward the roar, not for glory, but for the well-being of the team.

When Audie Murphy returned to the home front, he was ushered into his acting career by James Cagney, who invited the war hero to take a part in one of his upcoming movies. Other roles soon followed, but Murphy found that he could not simply rest on his laurels and enjoy the easy life of a Hollywood idol. Before long, he learned that he was suffering from what doctors now call Post Traumatic Stress Syndrome, which afflicts many soldiers after their wartime experience. When his emotional difficulties led to an addiction to sleeping pills, he found himself engaged in a battle every bit as tough as those he fought in France. With the same courage he summoned to win those battles, Murphy locked himself in a motel room for a week to cleanse his system of the drug and to prepare for a new phase of his life.

Still the caring big brother of all U.S. soldiers, Murphy spoke publicly of his problems in order to raise awareness of such an important, yet unknown issue. He wanted the returning Korean and Vietnam War veterans to receive the assistance they would need to overcome the traumatic effects of battle fatigue that he himself had overcome. He challenged the government to spend more time and money studying the causes and possible treatments of all the physical and mental ailments that plagued those who had fought for their country.

In a life that was cut short when he was only forty-six, Audie Murphy had lived several lifetimes. Neither the perils of war nor substance abuse would prevent him from accomplishing even more. Only a fluke would do that. On May 28, 1971, a plane carrying Murphy and several others became lost in the fog during a severe rainstorm and crashed into the side of a mountain near Roanoke, Virginia. Ten days later, Audie Murphy was buried with full military honors in Arlington National Cemetery. To every American he left a vital legacy of unflinching courage combined with altruistic selflessness to protect others. And Americans have not forgotten that legacy. Each year, only President John F. Kennedy's gravesite is visited more often than Audie Murphy's.

❧ DO IT FOR YOUR COMMUNITY

Unlike the earth-shattering roar of World War II, which was impossible to ignore, many people resolutely closed their ears to the steady and insidious roar of racism for centuries. In the United States, the oppression endured by African Americans continued almost unabated until the mid-1950s. In 1955, however, a single spark ignited what would evolve into the Civil Rights Movement, when an unexpected heroine committed an act of stoical and dignified civil disobedience. A quiet and reserved tailor's assistant named Rosa Parks started it all one winter afternoon when a white bus driver picked a fight with her because she simply wanted to ride peacefully home after a long day's work. The driver quickly discovered that he had challenged the wrong woman.

Rosa Louise McCauley was born and raised in Alabama by her schoolteacher mother, who stressed the importance of academic achievement to the young Rosa, instilling in her daughter a sense of pride in herself and her race. At age eleven, Rosa enrolled in the Montgomery Industrial School for Girls. There, she determined to give herself every possible advantage by tackling her schoolwork diligently. The path to independence, Rosa's mother had insisted, lay in the direction of self-empowerment.

In 1932, Rosa married Raymond Parks, a barber active in local civil rights groups. Rosa and Raymond shared much in common, as they both believed that the people of their race deserved a better life. To help put food on the table, Rosa Parks worked as a seamstress and a housekeeper, but her passion remained the pursuit of civil rights. In 1943, she began to work for the National Association for the Advancement of Colored People (NAACP), serving as a secretary for a time, then as a youth counselor. In the latter role, she says: "I was training them the proper way to integrate public facilities… I was telling them how to act if they were arrested."

Ironically, on December 1, 1955, Rosa Parks found herself under arrest. Riding the bus home from work that day, she refused to budge when the driver ordered her and three other African Americans to stand up so that a white passenger who had just boarded could sit. The segregation laws at the time mandated a separate section in the back of each bus for African American passengers. Parks had taken a seat in the first row of the "black section," but the driver had decided that, rather than allow one white rider to stand, the black section should give up one row: Rosa's row.

Having quietly suffered years of humiliation and discrimination, Rosa Parks knew the time had finally come to take a stand. Although the three other African Americans seated in the row (two women and one man) abandoned their seats without complaining, Rosa Parks politely refused. The driver became adamant and, when Parks would not relent, he threatened to have her arrested.

Rosa Parks responded to this threat with the bold reply: "You can do that." She was not going anywhere. Sensing trouble, several of the black passengers got off the bus, while all the white passengers remained. When the police arrived, they asked Parks whether she had defied the driver's orders. In the midst of an angry white crowd and facing arrest, Parks told them that she had refused to give up her seat and that she did not believe she should have to obey such an order. Hearing that, the police placed her under arrest and removed her from the bus.

The next day, her plight made front-page news. A meeting of several area ministers and citizens convened at a local church to discuss possible courses of action. The young pastor who spearheaded the meeting was a certain Dr. Martin Luther King. Parks related the details of her ordeal to those who attended. Three days later, her case went to trial, where a judge found her guilty but assessed no fine. While that had seemed to end the matter, the real drama was yet to unfold.

On the day of her trial, African Americans throughout Montgomery boycotted the bus lines, choosing to walk or find some other means of transportation. That one-day protest achieved such a profound effect that the black community decided to continue the boycott until they won their rights. The protest lasted for 382 days, ending only after the U.S. Supreme Court ruled segregation on city buses unlawful. The victory marked the first major blow struck by African Americans in their efforts to improve civil rights. Rosa Parks, whose unflinching courage ignited the cause, reflected on the event by saying, "I don't recall that I felt anything great about it. It didn't feel like a victory, actually. There still had to be a great deal to do."

Those words still sadly hold true, but Parks never flinched from her duty to the community, continuing her activism by lending her support to civil rights acts wherever she could. Despite the threats and hate mail she received after the boycott, she pressed onward, engaging in countless activities that she hoped would make a difference in the community, including creation of the Rosa and Raymond Parks Institute for Self-Development. The Institute provides worthwhile activities for young people, including cross-country bus tours designed to educate them about the history of the civil rights movement by retracing the Underground Railroad.

Over the years, Parks has continued her work with the NAACP, maintaining the same focus she had developed prior to her landmark bus ride: the elimination of inequity one case at a time. She still receives mail from people all over the country, thanking her for putting her courage behind her beliefs. Her quiet strength in the face of injustice made things go right, not just for one community, but for all communities in the country.

♣ Do It for the World

Many people pursue invention and discovery in order to attain money and fame. Others, however, simply dream of solving nature's puzzles for the sheer thrill of it. When research results in a discovery that can change the entire course of civilization, the work takes on an even higher level of meaning.

Textbooks list among Marie Curie's accomplishments the discovery of radium and invention of the first mobile X-ray machine. They also recognize her as the first woman to receive the Nobel Prize for science, an award she received twice in her lifetime. While Curie's tireless efforts in the laboratory resulted in significant scientific gains for mankind, the story often not revealed in textbooks involves her courage to forge ahead, even after the road became dangerous. Marie Curie's life offers a striking lesson in integrity and bravery in the face of hardship.

Born in Warsaw, Poland, in 1867, Marie Sklodowska began her life in humble surroundings. Her mother died at an early age, and her father could not support the family. As a result, she and her sisters took jobs in order to survive. Young Marie had the good fortune to land a position as a tutor for a family in a nearby town, a job that gave her the chance to earn her bread using her strongest muscle: her brain. She made enough money to help her struggling father and her sister Bronya, who had moved to Paris to study medicine. Before long, Marie joined her sister in Paris, where she studied mathematics and physics at the Sorbonne. By 1894, she had earned degrees in both disciplines.

After graduation, Marie remained in Paris to study magnetism, agreeing to share laboratory space with another young scientist named Pierre Curie. The two made a good match, and their mutual love of science soon blossomed into romance and marriage.

Working together, Marie and Pierre were introduced by a colleague to to a new concept in physics that Marie dubbed "radioactivity," a subject she pursued for her doctoral thesis. Fascinated by this new field, she devised, with help from Pierre, a method to measure the strength of the radiation emitted from uranium. The Curies' research eventually led them to discover two spontaneously radiating elements, which they named radium and polonium, the latter after Marie's native country.

In order to identify the properties of these elements, they set about isolating them, a task that proved long and arduous. Despite their huge commitment of time and money, and the lack of assurance that their work would pay off, Marie remained adamant about pressing forward. Four years later their research bore fruit when the Curies won the 1903 Nobel Prize in physics for their discovery of radium. The money that came with the award would keep the couple in a good financial position for the foreseeable future.

Then, in 1906, just as their life and work seemed perfectly on track, the unthinkable happened—Pierre was killed by a passing wagon on the streets of Paris. The freak accident left Marie shattered, her entire world turned upside down.

When offered the directoral position that her husband had been slated to fill at the Sorbonne's Physics Laboratory, Madame Curie, still in mourning and in complete emotional turmoil, made an incredibly courageous decision: she would accept the job, and continue the work that she and Pierre had begun. In the process, she would become the first woman director of a major research laboratory. With her personal life a scarred memory, she threw all her time and energy into her work, becoming a professor at the Sorbonne in 1908.

Her continued research into radium earned her a second Nobel Prize, this time for chemistry, in 1911.

Determined to apply her scientific discoveries to medicine, Madame Curie now turned her attention to the use of X-rays. She became the director of the scientific department of the Radium Institute in 1918 and dedicated the rest of her life to researching the chemistry of radioactive materials and their potential medical applications. Her research produced the further revelation that radiation kills human cells. While she realized that this discovery could lead to medical breakthroughs, she also understood that it posed a threat to her. Curie had been working with radioactive substances her entire adult life. If radiation killed human tissue, what might these compounds be doing to her own body? Now, Curie faced yet another difficult decision: should she play it safe and abandon her current research, or should she continue along this promising path of inquiry despite her concerns?

Curie elected to investigate the possibility of treating diseased human cells with radiation. During World War I, she designed the first mobile X-ray machine and personally implemented its use on the front lines in cases where French soldiers could not be moved to hospitals.

Curie continued her research with X-rays and other types of radiation, despite the fact that her own health had begun to deteriorate. On July 4, 1934, Curie died of leukemia, which had been caused by her protracted exposure to radiation. She may, in fact, have been the first person to die as a result of radiation poisoning. Despite her apprehensions of this eventuality, the knowledge that her work could save millions of lives and make possible an array of technological innovations had persuaded her to keep going.

One of the most brilliant scientists who ever lived, Marie Curie confronted intimidating obstacles that might have scared off a less courageous person. Losing her husband, with whom she had shared so much of her life and work, could have easily plunged her into debilitating despair. Then, when she found her own health imperiled by her work, she could have walked away from it all. But adversity only strengthened her determination to benefit the world. Her courage made things go right for millions of people because her work and life taught so much about the beneficial and harmful effects of radiation.

♣ COURAGE AND THE NEW MURPHY'S LAW

When we run away from life's challenges, we assure ourselves of mediocrity and condemn ourselves to a life of looking back and wondering, "What if?" By committing ourselves to a few basic tenets, we can ensure that we will be ready, willing and able to meet life's challenges head on. All of the individuals profiled in this chapter embody these maxims:

- ♣ **Lesson 1: Overcome Your Initial Fears**. Marliese Mitchell could have let fear for her career cause her to turn a blind eye to the situation she discovered in Southeast Asia. Have you ever found yourself in a situation where doing the right thing involved great personal risk? If so, did you act bravely, or did you let fear of consequences immobilize you? Do you let fear control your actions, or do you control your fear with courage and resolve? Although few of us will face extreme and dangerous situations, we must still find courage within ourselves to run toward, rather than away from, the roar.

♣ **Lesson 2: Listen to Your Inner Voice.** When John Hockenberry found himself physically challenged, he did not resort to self-pity but redoubled his efforts to prove he could do anything an able-bodied reporter could do. Do you unswervingly follow your inner convictions or do the doubts of others hold you back? If your friends, family, or colleagues express misgivings about your abilities, do you acquiesce to their opinion? Have you ever abandoned a difficult uphill path in favor of cruising effortlessly downhill—even though you sensed great rewards at the top of the mountain? When the going gets tough, the tough keep going. Let your empowering inner voice silence your critics.

♣ **Lesson 3: Draw Inspiration from Others.** Audie Murphy did not act out of a desire for personal glory, but out of love for his fellow soldiers, whose well-being inspired his courage. Have you ever risked your own security or reputation for the sake of others? Does your courage arise from self-preservation or from the desire to preserve the lives and work of others? Do your allegiances include those around you or only yourself? Whenever you find yourself in a taxing situation, remember that you can make things go right by thinking of those who depend on your courage and who, in return, will support you in your time of need.

♣ **Lesson 4: Maintain Your Dignity.** Rosa Parks did not rant and rave over injustice, she reacted calmly and with dignity. Have you ever found yourself reacting to an injustice impulsively, perhaps even violently? Does anger make you behave in an undignified manner? If so, think of the dignified Rosa Parks, who proved the value of quiet, steadfast courage. When something in your life or work goes wrong, don't get mad, just keep running toward the roar with the conviction that losing your dignity will only make matters worse.

♣ **Lesson 5: Move Forward with Persistence.** Marie Curie kept going when fainter-hearted scientists would have quit. Do you easily halt when personal setbacks or dangers arise in your life or work? How many times have you rationalized a change in direction because your original plan proved to take more courage and determination than you could muster? Sometimes you do need to change course, but whenever you feel you should, ask yourself whether doing so provides the easy way out. Quite often, the hard way, if it is the right way, will pay off in the long run.

These tenets form the foundation of the first rule of *The New Murphy's Law*: Run Toward the Roar. Once you learn to face up to your fears and confront them head on, you will find a whole new world of opportunity opening up to you.

Rule 2

Don't Just Communicate, Connect

"Good communication is as stimulating as black coffee and just as hard to sleep after."

Anne Morrow Lindbergh

♣ FEED THE WORLD

In 1984, a relatively unknown Irish musician brought to light one of history's most horrific episodes of human suffering and inspired people of all nations to "feed the world." Bob Geldof, the leader of a 1970s rock group called The Boomtown Rats, had gained popularity among only a small, loyal group of fans in Ireland and the United Kingdom. Although the band enjoyed moderate success in the early days of "new wave" music, it had not achieved anything like world-wide prominence. Among his fans, however, Geldof had earned a reputation as a tireless and gregarious artist with boundless energy, both on stage and off. This energy would win him an admiring international audience, though not just for his music.

The breakthrough began on an October day in 1984, as the thirty-year-old Geldof sat watching a BBC broadcast in his London flat. The program included film footage shot in Ethiopia, where Africans lay dying by the thousands. Geldof was shocked to learn that the Ethiopians could not grow food of any kind; they were dying of starvation. With a record-breaking drought plaguing the African continent, hundreds of thousands of people would die if nothing happened to alter the situation.

The program affected Geldof like nothing else he had ever witnessed. By week's end, he was preparing to fly to Ethiopia to gauge for himself the severity of the Africans' plight. The horrific conditions he saw in Africa haunted him. He could not comprehend how one region of the world could suffer such a dearth of food, while others enjoyed such a surplus.

When he returned to England, Geldof determined that he must do something to alleviate the suffering he had seen in Africa. He knew, though, that he could not do much all by himself. He would need help—and a lot of it. Bob Geldof then set his sights on a goal that few would dare to even imagine: enlisting the whole planet in his efforts to save the Ethiopian people. Geldof needed to reach millions. More than that, he must motivate them to act, to do something immediate and tangible to rescue a dying people. How, though, could one rock musician accomplish such a monumental feat?

With the holiday season approaching, Geldof decided to grab the world's attention by pointing out the disparity between the joy so many people around the world relished at Christmastime and the horrible misery so many in Ethiopia endured. After all, he reasoned, Christmas is the season of giving, and the time of year when the "holiday spirit" often moves people to greater generosity than they may feel at other times. Geldof penned new lyrics to the tune of one of his band's old songs, converting it into a new Christmas message: "Do They Know It's Christmas?" The lyrics made an impassioned plea to the listener to "feed the world," to act on the belief that for suffering and starving Ethiopian people, "...the greatest gift they'll get this year is life."

Geldof's song proved moving and inspirational, but merely recorded by his own band, it would reach far too few people to make a real difference. How could he expand its influence to ignite worldwide action? The answer came when Geldof decided to enlist some of his British rock-star friends to join him in recording "Do They Know It's Christmas?" The group, dubbed Band Aid, included David Bowie, Phil Collins, Paul McCartney, U2, Sting and more than two dozen other superstar musicians who already enjoyed the international audience Geldof needed.

The stars recorded the song on November 25, 1984, just in time for Christmas. Record sales soared as the song hit the charts in nearly every country in the world and became one of the best-selling records in history, raising more than $11 million worldwide. Geldof insisted that every penny of the proceeds go to ease the famine in Ethiopia. Unlike many charitable efforts, the musicians received no stipends or expenses, and Geldof deducted no administrative costs from the fund. At Geldof's urging, all who participated in recording, distributing and promoting the song volunteered their time.

Many other countries around the world quickly caught the vision. Most notably, musicians in the United States formed USA for Africa to record "We Are the

World," while Canada's Northern Lights performed "Tears Are Not Enough." Soon, charitable groups of all types rushed to raise money specifically to combat the hunger in Ethiopia.

But Bob Geldof did not stop there. In May 1985, he planted the seeds for staging an unheard-of live, two-continent musical extravaganza. For a period of sixteen hours, some of the world's most famous musical acts appeared at Wembley Stadium in London and JFK Stadium in Philadelphia, performing free to benefit the starving people in Africa. On July 13, Live Aid aired across the globe as millions of viewers tuned in. Through donations and sponsorships associated with the event, more than $70 million was raised to directly benefit the cause that had begun in front of a television set in a London flat.

The overwhelming success of Band Aid and Live Aid earned Geldof a Nobel Peace Prize, and the rare honor of knighthood. More importantly, although the African crisis did fade, nearly fifteen years later Geldof's tune replays on the airwaves during the holiday season, reminding people of a time when the world came together to relieve the suffering of our fellow human beings. Through his song, Geldof still spreads a message of hope that the whole world can work together in harmony, and that, even without the luxury of great celebrity or unlimited financial resources, a person can make things go right by connecting with his audience.

Every day, each of us tries to communicate our thoughts and ideas to others. We speak on the telephone, fax memos, write letters, send e-mail and make presentations. But do our communications fully connect us with those to whom they're directed? Do we really get through to one another? Even when we do, does the right message get through, or some muddled version of our intended message?

DON'T JUST COMMUNICATE, CONNECT

Communication alone means nothing unless it forges a *connection*. Whether we seek to connect to a child, a lover, a team, or several million people, as Bob Geldof did, our efforts achieve little if they fail to connect us to our audience. Without connection, you cannot make things go right.

This chapter will introduce four bylaws for connection that you can incorporate into all your communication efforts:

FOUR BYLAWS FOR CONNECTION

1   Let Your Actions Speak Loudly

2   Speak Truthfully and Boldly

3   Listen as Hard as You Can

4   Keep Your Audience in Mind

Have you ever listened to another person's words but felt that his actions told a different story? How can you make sure that your own actions do not belie your words?

Did you ever believe in the soundness of a suggestion you wished to offer but felt too shy or too afraid to make it?

Do you routinely seek out the opinions of others? When they respond, do you listen objectively?

How do you connect with your audience when they seem to have lost interest in what you're trying to communicate?

The people whose stories you will encounter in this chapter have faced situations that challenged them to wrestle with and answer these questions. By heeding the lessons their stories reveal, so can you.

❧ LET YOUR ACTIONS SPEAK LOUDLY

In 1923, young Bill Havens' lifelong dream came true when he qualified to compete in the 1924 Olympic Games. In fact, Havens represented one of America's best prospects for a medal because he had established himself as a world-class contender in the singles and the four-man canoeing events.

Several months before he was scheduled to leave for Paris, the site of the 1924 Olympics, Havens' wife joyfully told him that he would soon fulfill another great dream: they were expecting a baby. Coincidentally, the baby was due smack dab in the middle of the two-week Olympic competition.

In the 1920s, traveling from the United States to Europe required a two-week voyage across the Atlantic on an ocean liner. With the trip there and back, and the two weeks of competition, Havens would be gone more than a month-and-a-half. If he went to Paris, he would almost certainly miss the birth of his child.

Bill Havens faced a quandary: two wonderful landmark events loomed before him, but he could not possibly attend both. When he asked his family and friends what he should do, they encouraged him to go and compete. He could win glory for himself and for his country and, after all, his child would be waiting for him when he returned home. His wife's doctor assured him that the pregnancy was progressing perfectly and that his wife and child would be fine. Even Mrs. Havens urged her husband to follow his dream of Olympic gold.

Still, Bill Havens spent many days deep in thought before he felt comfortable making his crucial decision. On the one hand, he would possibly win a medal but, on the other, one moment of glory paled in comparison to a mother's and a child's life. Finally, Havens chose: he would not go to Paris. Instead, he would stay home with his wife, by her bedside, and welcome their child into the world.

Bill Havens could have easily told his wife, "I love you, I'll be with you in spirit," then kissed her good-bye and boarded the boat. Instead, he chose to show her, and their unborn child, the sincerity of his love for them. On August 1, 1924, Bill's son was born—four days after the Paris Games concluded. If Havens had gone to the Olympics, he would have been aboard a ship in the middle of the Atlantic Ocean at the moment his son Frank came into the world.

Bill Havens felt he had made the right decision, but he could not keep himself from imagining, over the years, what it would have felt like to stand on the victory platform with the *Star Spangled Banner* playing and the crowd cheering. He sometimes doubted whether anyone cared about his sacrifice. In the long run, had what he'd done at home really mattered more than what he might have done in Paris?

In the summer of 1952, Bill Havens finally got his answer. That year the Olympics took place in Helsinki, Finland, and in the midst of the games, a telegram arrived at the Havens' home from Frank Havens. That telegram read:

"Dear Dad, Thanks for waiting around for me to get born in 1924. I'm coming home with the gold medal you should have won.... Your loving son, Frank."

Frank Havens had competed in the 10,000-meter singles canoeing event, one that his father might himself have won in 1924. When young Frank won Olympic gold, his first thought turned to his father, who had sacrificed the same glory in favor of his love for his family. Bill Havens' actions had spoken volumes about his values, and they connected him to his family and his fans more than any words or any lump of metal ever could. In the end, they made things go right.

🍀 SPEAK TRUTHFULLY AND BOLDLY

In October of 1860, eleven-year-old Grace Bedell made a singular contribution to our nation's history. A resident of the tiny village of Westfield, New York, not far from Buffalo, this curious girl was an astute observer of the people and events around her. She felt especially drawn to Abraham Lincoln, who was then making his first bid for the presidency. Grace had heard much about this well-spoken man who had won the Republican nomination, and she got her first glimpse of him when her father brought home his picture.

While studying Lincoln's photograph, Grace's lamp cast shadows around his face, obscuring his hollow cheeks. "Whiskers!" thought Grace, "How much better Abraham Lincoln would look if only he had more whiskers!" Undaunted by the thought of Lincoln's fame, Grace resolved to send him a letter offering her suggestion. She wrote, "I am a little girl, eleven years old, but I want you to be president of the United States very much. So I hope you won't think me very bold to write to such a great man as you are." She continued, "I have four brothers, and some of them will vote for you. If you will let your whiskers grow, I will try to get the others to vote for you." Grace asserted that with a beard, Lincoln "would look a great deal better for your face is so thin." A softer-looking Lincoln would, she reasoned, not frighten children, and would attract ladies to encourage their husbands to vote for him. Grace mailed her letter with a polite request that Lincoln answer it.

At that time, Abraham Lincoln received about fifty letters each day. His secretaries, John Hay and John Nicolay, reviewed all the correspondence and then passed along only those letters they deemed important. Hay happened to scan Grace's letter on the morning it arrived, and he found the suggestion fascinating. Nicolay, however, thought the note frivolous and insisted they toss it into the wastebasket. The two men debated the fate of the note for a time, neither willing to give in. The argument came to an end, however, when Mr. Lincoln walked into the room, overheard the discussion, and plucked the note from Hay's hand. A few days later, much to her surprise, Grace received a written reply from Lincoln thanking her for her advice. The note did not seem to promise he would accept it, however: "My dear little Miss,… As to the whiskers, having never worn any, do you not think people would call it a piece of silly affectation if I were to begin it now?"

Nevertheless, the idea of growing whiskers became firmly planted in Lincoln's mind, as did the source of that idea. As we know, Abraham Lincoln's campaign ended successfully, and he did indeed become the sixteenth president of the United States. In February 1861, the newly elected president made his way from Illinois to Washington to assume his new post at the White House, a travel route that took the train through New York State. Lincoln gave instructions for a special stop in Westfield. As usual, the townspeople turned out in droves to see their new president, and, naturally, young Grace Bedell stood among them.

As Lincoln exited the train, everyone recognized him by his tall and impressive stature, but something different about his appearance also caught their eye. The great man sported a set of whiskers that would become his trademark. After Lincoln quieted the crowd, he called out to inquire whether Grace Bedell was in the audience. When he learned that she was, he asked her to join him on the platform, where he publicly thanked her for her sound political advice and gave her a kiss. Grace assured him that he now possessed all the tools he needed to become the greatest president the country had ever known.

Grace Bedell, perhaps the youngest campaign adviser in the history of American politics, pursued a connection with a presidential candidate because she believed she could help him. We will never know whether or not the whiskers made all the difference in that election, but we do know that Grace did not allow herself to feel intimidated by the prestige or power of her audience—she chose, instead, to communicate a truthful and helpful message. Her precocious courage should encourage any of us who have ever felt afraid to speak out. For things to go right, you must speak truthfully and boldly.

☘ Listen As Hard As You Can

Many of us have, at one time or another, worked for a boss who formulates grand schemes, sets down regulations, and issues orders without ever explaining the reasoning behind his or her corporate decisions. As employees, we often feel compelled to accept the edicts of our boss because, after all, we have little choice in the matter. However, we may also perform the tasks demanded of us by such an employer only halfheartedly, simply because we must. Thinking the boss insensitive to our own needs, desires and aspirations, we do the work but steadily lose respect for the person giving the orders. Why should we respect such a boss or maintain any loyalty to the company? Communication may exist, but it flows only one way, and it never creates the sense of connection that enables people to work hard to make things go right for both themselves and their employer.

Sam Walton, the founder of the $50-billion Wal-Mart chain of retail stores, understood the value of forging a true connection with his employees, enabling the people who worked for him to act as if they were working for a family-owned enterprise. In fact, by doing so, Sam Walton won recognition as one of the most sincere and genuine executives in the history of corporate America. How did he do it? By using his eyes and ears more than his mouth.

Walton saw his associates (he never referred to them as employees) as partners rather than as resources to be deployed, used and disposed of. He put into action what most executives only talk about: valuing the people who actually do the work. Every Wal-Mart associate functioned as an integral member of the team, and they all knew it. They also eagerly accepted the challenge to do the best work they could. Mr. Sam, as his associates called him, offered each person an opportunity to become a part of something larger than him- or herself; his company embodied the concept of the "corporate family."

Although his "family" grew large, Sam Walton made extraordinary efforts to get to know as many of its members as he possibly could. Wal-Mart's 300,000 associates certainly knew him well enough to give him a nickname. Mr. Sam would routinely fly his twin-engine plane from store to store to meet his employees, sometimes without more than an hour's notice. Far from doing so to spy on his people, he went to listen to their concerns about the store, their customers and their own lives. He spent considerable time with his associates, offering advice on how individuals or stores could improve their weaknesses. Throughout his life, Walton demonstrated to his corporate family that he truly cared about the well-being and the opinions of each of them, whether they worked as store managers or clerks. Even after he became one of the wealthiest men in the country, Mr. Sam did not end his store-hopping campaigns.

By connecting so well with his associates, by listening to them as hard as he could, Mr. Sam also improved the welfare of his customers. The front-line workers in every Wal-Mart store understood the importance of giving all customers who walked through the front door the attention and respect they deserved. Taking a cue from the "boss," they listened carefully to each customer. They knew that Walton strongly believed in the customer as an equal partner in his company's success. As a result, Wal-Mart rejected the idea of price gouging, offering "everyday low prices" instead. The movement he spawned reduced gross profit margins in the industry from over 60 percent in the 1950s to 22 percent in the 1990s but, as he explained himself, the lower margins provided greater access to goods and services for those who needed them most.

At the time of his death, in April 1994, Mr. Sam had built the most successful retail business in American history. Years later, Wal-Mart continues to stand as the store of choice for millions of shoppers. Its success stems directly from the fact that Sam Walton took the time to make his associates feel appreciated and to instill in them the desire to do their best. He knew that by putting people first and listening to them with both ears, the bottom line would take care of itself. In short, by listening hard he helped make things go right.

🍀 KEEP YOUR AUDIENCE IN MIND

William J. Byron, S.J., the retired president of Catholic University and a distinguished professor of business ethics at Georgetown University, is a charismatic teacher, public speaker and writer who never forgets the purpose of his communication. When he retired from university administration he became interested in the plight of workers who were being laid off in their middle-aged years during a decade of harsh corporate downsizing. William J. Byron, known to friends as Father Bill, understood the depression and desperation people suffered when they lost jobs that they had assumed were secure. He wanted to do something that would help displaced workers keep their hope for the future alive, but what could one man do?

Byron knew that in order to do the most good, he needed to know as much as possible about the feelings and needs of those he wished to reach. Supported by a Lilly Foundation grant, Father Bill spent a year traveling the country, talking with hundreds of men and women in their fifties and sixties who had suddenly lost top-paying jobs. This research resulted in *Finding Work Without Losing Heart*, a book full of wisdom and comfort that showed people how they could triumph despite the most depressing setbacks to their lives and careers. While the book attracted a great deal of national media attention, one brief radio interview inspired a vital connection that fulfilled Father Bill's purpose in writing his book.

"I was sitting at my desk at Georgetown," Father Bill recalls, "when I got a phone call out of the blue from a fellow in Chicago. It turned out he had been downsized out of a top executive job with a major insurance company and suddenly found himself with a huge mortgage, two kids in college, and no hope of finding a job that could support his family. 'I began drinking too much,' he said, 'and I took out my frustration on my wife. We separated, and I hit bottom. In fact, I'd bought a .38, loaded it, and sat on my bed in my squalid apartment contemplating suicide. The radio was on, and some interviewer was talking with a priest about a book he had just published. His words gave me hope for the first time in months.'"

Father Bill shakes his head as he describes the caller's suffering. "The fellow unloaded the gun, lay awake all night, then went to Barnes & Noble before the doors opened. He bought my book, read it, joined Alcoholics Anonymous, apologized to his wife, went to a job counselor, and polished his résumé. The last I heard he'd gotten a good job and put his life back together. Saving that one life made writing my book worthwhile." Father Bill's book didn't just communicate—it connected. And it did so because it spoke directly to his intended audience.

♣ CONNECTION AND THE NEW MURPHY'S LAW

Oftentimes, we make the mistake of believing that simply because we have made a statement, because we have broadcast our ideas to the world, we have communicated. In reality, however, we have fulfilled only the smallest, simplest step in the process of fully connecting with our audience. Whether we hope to convey information to only one person or to the entire world, the lessons remain the same. To make things go right, you must:

> ♣ **Lesson 1: Commit to a Cause**. As Bob Geldof's story exemplifies, communication and connection begin with commitment. Do you *really* believe in the message you hope to convey to family, friends and coworkers? Have you clearly defined the *goals* of your communication? Do your words, both written and spoken, spring from an honest desire to improve relationships and benefit the recipients of your messages as much, or more, than they do yourself? If you can answer yes to these questions, you stand a

far greater chance of reaching—and connecting with—your intended audiences.

♣ **Lesson 2: Couple Your Words with Action.** Bill Havens' values drove actions that spoke louder than words. You may appreciate the need for "talking the talk," but do you back up your communication by "walking the walk"? Have you ever made the mistake of expecting those with whom you hope to connect to "do as I say, not as I do"? If you have, commit to making actions that prove the value of your communication.

♣ **Lesson 3: Speak Boldly and Truthfully, or Forever Hold Your Peace.** Grace Bedell's courage teaches much more than that the truth often comes from the mouths of babes. Have you ever let your feelings of intimidation or shyness or a lack of courage prevent you from saying what you mean and meaning what you say? Do you ever hold your peace because you expect or assume that someone else, perhaps someone with more authority or more eloquence, will do it for you? Have you ever looked back on a missed opportunity to connect with someone and said, "If I had only spoken up when I had the chance"? If so, remember that others respect those who strive boldly to tell the truth.

♣ **Lesson 4: Use Your Ears More Than Your Tongue.** Sam Walton received more messages than he conveyed. In your conversations and correspondences do you ask a lot of questions? Do you ever find yourself thinking about what you will say next while other people are talking? Do you grow impatient when the people you talk to start rambling or repeating themselves? Whenever you feel such impulses, remind yourself that God gave us two ears and one mouth for a reason. Listen twice as much as you talk.

♣ **Lesson 5: Tailor Your Message to Your Audience.** Father Bill got to know his audience before he communicated his advice. Do you take time to get to know the feelings, hopes, or fears of those with whom you wish to communicate *before* you start talking or writing? Do you use the same words in every situation, regardless of differences between one audience and another? Can you honestly say you try to put yourself in the other person's shoes when you engage that person in conversation? If you gain intimate knowledge of your audience, you will find yourself choosing your words more carefully to forge a firm connection every time you communicate.

By taking time to contemplate these lessons and to ask yourself the questions they imply, you will move beyond the position of the communicator who sends out messages hoping that people will receive them. You will instead become more of a connector—a person who builds the relationships with others that help make things go right.

Rule 3

Make Change Your Constant Ally

"There is nothing in this world constant but inconstancy."

Jonathan Swift

♣ THE EYE OF THE STORM

We all undergo change constantly. Sometimes the change results from well-laid plans: a move to a new home or a long-anticipated job change. Quite often, however, change can strike suddenly and surprisingly: the unanticipated loss of a job, or an unexpected illness. Whatever the source of change in our lives, it usually causes stress, and our ability to handle that stress greatly influences whether or not we weather the change successfully. Those who stand the best chance of making things go right recognize that change, even disruptive change, not only will inevitably occur but will also offer an opportunity to grow.

Andy Grove, currently Chief Executive Officer (CEO) of Intel Corporation, has frequently demonstrated the value of making change your ally. Born in Hungary, Grove and his family fled the tyranny of Soviet oppression for the promise of the United States, arriving in New York City penniless, yet excited and enthusiastic to begin their new life.

While moving to a new country with an entirely different culture and language would overwhelm some people, it barely phased Andy Grove, who immediately immersed himself in the new life his parents had given him. Through diligence and perseverance, Grove overcame the language barrier and worked his way through the City University of New York and, eventually, the University of California at Berkeley, where he received a Ph.D. in physics. Success came easily in business too, as Grove rose to become one of the world's pre-eminent industry and technology leaders, and one of the designers of a revolutionary computer chip. No one could deny that Andy Grove had adapted to change like a chameleon. Things always went right for him.

Then, in the fall of 1994, something went very wrong for Andy Grove. At fifty-eight, he learned that he had prostate cancer. After a series of tests, Grove's urologist phoned him at the office with news that would alter Andy Grove's life forever: "Andy, you have a tumor. It's mainly on the right side; there's a tiny bit on the left. It's a moderately aggressive one."

When first diagnosed with a life-threatening disease, many people bury their heads in the sand, hoping the problem will disappear on its own. At first, Grove did just that. The initial fear of death prompted him to assume a passive position, consigning responsibility for managing this drastic change in his life to the "experts."

Soon, however, he became restless and disappointed in himself for not applying the life lessons he had learned as an immigrant, a business leader and a scientist. Why couldn't he take charge of the situation and make change his ally as he had done so many times before? Wasn't he the real expert about his own future? Opting for a brief sabbatical from his job to evaluate his situation, Grove determined to take charge of his own survival. With a storm raging into his life, he chose to occupy the eye of that storm and figure out what to do about it.

From that point on, Grove began to make things go right. He developed a new daily routine that included in-depth searches in medical databases, online resources and medical magazines for any and all information about prostate cancer. He applied his experience and knowledge as a world-class researcher to a new topic, tracking down articles and research reports that he passed on to the experts who were overseeing his care. Nightly, Grove's wife trekked to the library for copies of the articles that her husband had catalogued during the day. Grove got second opinions, third opinions and real-life accounts from others who had overcome prostate cancer.

Then, he combined all his research, his own test results, information from the ongoing conversations he was conducting with prostate cancer patients, oncologists, surgeons and other doctors, and created a chart of all the possible treatment options, their side effects and the probabilities of recurrence. Just as he had organized resources to address other changes in his life, he applied his analytical skills to help him decide how to tackle his disease and chart a course toward success.

Ultimately, Andy Grove landed upon a new, but promising, treatment option. It involved implanting eight pin-like tubes near the tumor, through which doctors would insert radioactive "seeds" for a short period of time. After receiving this high-dose radiation treatment, Grove underwent twenty-eight daily doses of external radiation, which took no more than a few minutes each. He would walk into a local hospital at 7:30 in the morning and then arrive at work for a full day by 8:30.

Six months after the start of treatment, Andy Grove reclaimed his life—100 percent cancer-free. By refusing to allow external forces to control his fate, Grove demonstrated the benefits of making change an ally rather than an enemy. As he continues his research and the ongoing process of managing change brought on by cancer, sharing his progress through interviews, speeches and counseling, Grove proves true the old cliché that "whatever doesn't kill you, only makes you stronger." Unquestionably, prostate cancer could have killed Andy Grove had he not chosen to use his affliction to make himself stronger.

The winds of change blow through our lives daily, whether long-awaited and expected or unforeseen, as in the case of Andy Grove. Our ability to define these challenges as opportunities makes it possible for us to control how our futures unfold. These challenges arise in four basic forms:

FOUR WINDS OF CHANGE

1 Unanticipated Change

2 Imposed Change

3 Self-Instigated Change

4 Anticipated Change

Has an unwelcome change ever blindsided you? When you find yourself facing such a change, do you avoid thinking about the situation? Or do you tackle the life-altering event head on, seeking a way to conquer it?

How do you react when events impose immediate change on your life? Can you think on your feet and find a way to make something positive out of the situation? Can you quickly adjust to your new circumstances?

Have you ever deliberately planned a major change? Can you organize and implement the alteration in your life smoothly?

Even when you anticipate a change, does that change still cause you discomfort or stress?

In this chapter, we will explore some of the different ways change may enter our lives. The people whose stories we will encounter exemplify how to handle potentially trying situations with grace and wisdom. Some of them were forced to accept change, while others sought it out, but each chose to make things go right by stepping up to the challenges and welcoming the opportunities they offered.

♣ Unanticipated Change

History has a way of lionizing individuals who have achieved excellence or somehow bettered the world through science, policy, humanitarianism or the arts. While many historical figures deserve praise in these fields, we should not make the mistake of believing that our heroes calculated every move, deliberately fitting together each piece of life's puzzle. In reality, many of our most beloved heroes faced gut-wrenching change they neither expected nor wanted, but when that happened, they did not let circumstances prevent them from reaching their goals.

Ludwig van Beethoven is perhaps the most recogniz- able name in the history of music. Born in 1770 to a court musician and singer in Bonn, Germany, the young

Beethoven did not live in the lap of luxury, even though he displayed a prodigious musical talent. At age eight he gave his first public performance as a pianist, and by age eleven he was methodically studying performance and composition with a local music teacher.

Despite his tremendous gift as a musician and the praise he received from others, Beethoven endured much abuse at the hands of his ill-tempered and domineering father, who would force his son to play upon demand, either for the amusement of his friends or to discipline the boy. Young Beethoven also suffered the frequent violent outbursts that came whenever his father returned home in a drunken stupor. As the elder Beethoven tried to reconcile his jealousy of his son's talent with his desire for him to succeed, he grew even more unpredictably violent.

The son quietly turned his suffering inward and concentrated on his music. In 1787, he left for Vienna to study with the masters. Untutored in the social graces and unkempt in appearance, he did not fit in with the sophisticated Viennese musicians. But he persevered, refining his art with such luminaries as Mozart and Haydn, and quickly developing a reputation as a brilliant piano virtuoso. Just as his star began to rise, however, the unexpected death of his mother forced him to return to Bonn, where he assumed the responsibility of helping his family through a period of prolonged struggle.

Returning to Vienna a few years later, Beethoven resumed lessons with Haydn, and also sought out other prominent composers of the time—among them Albrechtsberger and Salieri—for guidance. Soon he was performing his own compositions at the piano. His talent was obvious, and he began to establish his reputation as a master of the first rank. His symphonic compositions soon followed, galvanizing both the cognoscenti and the public alike. Capturing the passion of emerging democratic and romantic ideals of individualism in his music, he quickly achieved universal acclaim. The demand for his music made it possible for Beethoven to command substantial commissions from the aristocratic patrons to whom he dedicated his compositions. Not only had he arrived as a renowned musician, he had gained the financial stability that had always eluded him. The unhappiness and indignity of his childhood became distant memories.

However, just as everything began to go right, something began to go very wrong: during his thirties, Beethoven started to experience difficulties with his hearing. An initially subtle disorder steadily worsened until, within a couple of years, he could hear only distorted sounds and could not hear soft or loud sounds at all. The cruel irony of the situation—the musician who could no longer hear his own music—was not lost on Beethoven, who sank into a deep despair, fearing that he would lose both his passion and his livelihood.

Although he could not continue to perform with confidence, Beethoven did not fold up his music and retire to obscurity. Instead, he summoned strength to confront his depression and use this change to his advantage. As he wrote to a friend: "You must think of me as being as happy as it is possible to be on this earth—not unhappy. No! I cannot endure it. I will seize Fate by the throat. It will not wholly conquer me! Oh, how beautiful it is to live—and live a thousand times over!"

Beethoven knew that despite his hearing loss, he could and must still compose. After a brief sojourn in the country on the advice of his doctors, who hoped that the quiet country life might ease his hearing problems, he threw himself into an even more complex and passionate approach to composing.

This renewed effort resulted in Beethoven's Third Symphony, the *Eroica*, which took the music world by storm—as did his revocation of the piece's dedication to Napoleon. He made this bold action after learning that Napoleon had declared himself emperor in betrayal of the principles of the French Revolution, which Beethoven fervently supported.

Paradoxically, as his hearing continued to deteriorate, Beethoven's music flourished. He completed two of his greatest works—the Fifth and Sixth Symphonies—in 1808, during a period of intense pain. This period of remarkable creativity culminated in 1823, with the composition of the Ninth Symphony. Inspired by Schiller's great poem the *Ode to Brotherhood*, the Ninth Symphony embodied the ideals of the enlightenment, from the Declaration of Independence to the burgeoning science of the industrial age. Written by an almost stone-deaf composer, it is generally considered one of the greatest works of art ever completed.

When Beethoven died four years later, more than 30,000 people attended his funeral. Then, as now, Beethoven commanded reverential respect. He demonstrated how an unswerving belief in the power of the human spirit can transform the threat of change into a catalyst for greatness.

Had Beethoven given in to his hearing loss, he and the world would have lost an important marker in the path of human progress. Fortunately, nature had bestowed on him a gift every bit as precious as his musical genius: perseverance in the face of devastating change. Refusing to allow his talent to wither and die because of an arbitrary stroke of bad luck, he transformed the threat of change into an even more powerful resolve to achieve.

♣ IMPOSED CHANGE

Responses to change don't have to produce a great work of art to have impact. Robert Landau's story is a case in point.

Sometimes other people or circumstances impose change on our lives. During the late 1980s and early 1990s, thousands of workers found themselves "downsized" out of their jobs, and few, especially Landau, saw it coming.

Landau had risen to the position of advertising director for a footwear company, when, in 1993, the firm took a chainsaw to its payroll. A younger man might have bounced back quickly from such an imposed change in circumstances, but when the middle-aged Landau got laid off, he found that most potential employers preferred younger executives. He could not find another job. Fortunately, he had planned ahead and built up a sufficient nest-egg to support himself comfortably without working. Like others whose identity and personal sense of worth are wrapped up in their jobs, Landau found himself wondering, "What should I do with the rest of my life?"

Five years later, still unemployed, Landau had not yet found an answer—he spent his time doing what so many people do when they stay home during the day: watching television. Tuning in to the *Oprah Winfrey Show* one day, he heard Oprah pitch her "Angel Network," a campaign she had launched to encourage people to reach out and make small differences in the lives of others. Landau later said he was inspired by the idea that one person could make a difference. Although things were not going right for him, they were going even worse for others, so he decided that he would make good use of his abundant time to see what difference he could make in someone else's life.

What to do? Well, he decided to do what he knew how to do. He applied his knowledge of advertising and the shoe business to helping people. Landau had seen homeless men and women limping around in worn-down, ill-fitting shoes. Believing he might do a little something to ease their discomfort, he established a World Wide Web site where the public could log on and donate a pair of shoes to a homeless person.

In the first two months of its existence, Landau's website (shoesonthenet.com) collected more than 18,000 pairs of new shoes for homeless people across the United States. To distribute the shoes, Landau worked personally with a program for the homeless run through the Pine Street Inn in Boston. Lyndia Downie, vice president of the program, enthusiastically supported his efforts. She saw so many people served by her program delighted when they received the small gift of a brand-new pair of shoes. Usually, she explained, her clients rummaged through piles of old, used shoes, and were lucky if they found a pair that almost fit their feet. In fact, after putting on her new pair of shoes, one woman told Downie that merely owning something new made her feel more normal, more like everybody else.

Just as Oprah Winfrey's "Angel Network" had caught his attention two months earlier, Robert Landau's "shoesonthenet" program caught the attention of Oprah early in 1998, and soon the television star invited him to appear on her show to explain the work to which he had dedicated himself. On the show, Landau announced a new aspect of his World Wide Web drive. Through his experiences working with the homeless, Landau had discovered that not only did many people need new footwear, they also needed socks. So, he launched a "white socks drive" in conjunction with his shoe campaign. Since most homeless people walk a lot, they often succumb to foot problems, problems that good shoes and clean socks can help alleviate. Landau specifically asked for white socks because the colored dye from tinted socks could aggravate some foot conditions.

In the twenty-four hours after his appearance on Oprah Winfrey's show, visits to Landau's website increased by approximately 20 percent. Now he plans to continue his charitable campaign indefinitely: "We are looking for 30,000 to 50,000 pairs (of shoes), but we will be running the campaign until we exhaust the industry."

In addition to perpetuating "shoesonthenet," Robert Landau hopes to include other philanthropic enterprises in his future plans, as he transforms the change in life imposed on him into a career of making positive changes in the lives of others. He vows that he will not return to the corporate world, but will, instead, continue to develop his new-found career in social service. As he explains, "I have had the other wealth. The most important wealth is the kind you give to other people"—and the kind you receive in return. Robert Landau had transformed the bad hand dealt him by others into an opportunity for personal growth and achievement.

♣ SELF-INSTIGATED CHANGE

The life of Albert Schweitzer provides testimony to the idea that we can control the direction our lives take, even when drastic changes occur. Schweitzer was born in 1875 in a tiny country village in Alsace, then part of Germany. Gifted with many talents, he displayed a particular knack for the humanities. Schweitzer studied literature and music passionately, devoting considerable time to mastering the organ under the tutelage of some of Europe's finest teachers. Schweitzer entered college in 1893, where he broadened his interests to include philosophy and theology. In 1899, he earned a Doctorate in Philosophy from the University of Strasbourg, and later studied at the Sorbonne and the University of Berlin.

Upon concluding his studies, Schweitzer accepted a position as a pastor at St. Nicholai's Church. Throughout the next several years, he received numerous prestigious appointments, including principal of St. Thomas College in Strasbourg, curate at St. Nicholai, and faculty member at the University of Strasbourg. In addition to his work in academia, he also wrote prolifically, penning works on subjects of personal interest to him, including his most celebrated book, *The Quest for the Historical Jesus*. The lives and work of the philosopher Immanuel Kant and the great composer Johann Sebastian Bach also inspired Schweitzer's literary efforts. Amazingly, though, despite all his accomplishments, Albert Schweitzer had barely begun to make a difference in the world.

Throughout his early adulthood, Schweitzer had begun to envision a life very different from the one he had been living. He became preoccupied with the notion that despite his prowess in the humanities, he should seek a greater purpose to fulfill. Even as he cemented his reputation as a brilliant theologian, philosopher, musician and writer, he fervently believed that his future lay far afield from these areas.

In 1904, Schweitzer's plans crystallized for him when he read an article in the Paris Missionary Society's journal urging physicians to relocate to the French colony of Gabon on a mission of mercy. Conflicting emotions ran through his mind as he considered this desperate plea. He did not question for a second his desire to go to Gabon and help out in whatever way he could, but he had no medical training. For most of us, this problem would represent more than a stumbling block, it would look like a brick wall. But Albert Schweitzer saw a window of opportunity, not a wall. He now knew what he wanted to do; he just needed to figure out a way to do it.

MAKE CHANGE YOUR CONSTANT ALLY

In Albert Schweitzer's next sermon at St. Nicholai's Church, he shared the depth of his new feelings with his congregation, eloquently stressing the need to assist those mired in poverty and deprivation: "And now, when you speak about missions, let this be your message: We must make atonement for all the terrible crimes we read of in the newspapers. We must make atonement for the still worse ones, which we do not read about in the papers; crimes that are shrouded in silence."

Soon thereafter, Schweitzer wrote to his family and friends to inform them that he planned to study medicine. He had spent enough time speaking and writing about the importance of living a selfless life; the time had come to start living one. Schweitzer would work toward becoming a physician, and then he would serve the poor for the remainder of his life. His loved ones and colleagues tried to dissuade him from what they saw as a hasty and silly decision, but he ignored every plea and letter beseeching him to reconsider his plans, believing with St. James that "Faith, if it has no works, is dead." For Schweitzer, such change was required to find personal fulfillment and test the validity and meaning of his life.

In January 1905, the thirty-year-old Schweitzer shed his former life and entered medical school. It would take him eight long years to receive his degree, years he invested with the same blood, sweat and tears he had invested in all his endeavors. At the age of thirty-eight, Schweitzer graduated from medical school with a specialization in tropical medicine and surgery.

Although Schweitzer attained his first goal, he soon found that his carefully planned course would not run smoothly from that point on. Although he had intended to work for the same Paris Missionary Society whose journal had inspired him to change his life, he found that the agency would not accept him because of his strong religious views. Members of the Society feared that rather than acting only as a physician, Schweitzer would likely feel compelled to advocate his own religious beliefs.

Despite this setback, Schweitzer stayed the course, proposing a unique offer to the Society: he and his wife Helene, a trained nurse, would spearhead an effort to raise funds to build, stock and maintain a hospital in Gabon. The Society need contribute nothing. After some consternation within the Society, including the resignation of one key member, Schweitzer's offer was accepted, and, in March of 1913, he and his wife left for Africa to build the hospital. They began treating their patients in a small ramshackle shed that had once been a chicken coop, but expanded the facilities at every opportunity. Eventually, the hospital could accommodate thousands of patients who would otherwise not have received the care they needed.

Over the remaining years of his life, Schweitzer continued to serve the greater good, with his work ultimately earning him the Nobel Peace Prize in 1953. In addition to working in his hospital, he later lent his efforts in support of nuclear disarmament and protecting the environment. His efforts were not without personal risk—they often put him in direct conflict with political and military authorities seeking to exploit Africa and eliminate voices of dissent. Albert Schweitzer did not stop his humanitarian work until he died at the age of ninety. At that time, his daughter Rhena assumed responsibility for the hospital, which still serves the needy today.

Schweitzer made a career and life change more drastic than most of us will ever contemplate. He left behind a life of fame and prestige to pursue a personal vision of success requiring a dramatic transformation and retooling. His story shows us how we can each take charge of our own futures, whatever our personal vision of success might be, and initiate change on our own terms.

♣ ANTICIPATED CHANGE

Success in business can prove elusive. Nerves of steel, intelligence, and refined people skills provide just a few of the elements you need to guide a company to dominance in the marketplace. Regardless of your own aptitudes, you may never grasp the brass ring, especially if you don't have one indispensable quality: the ability to foresee change and to react to it before it even arrives. Lee Iacocca possessed that quality.

Born to two Italian immigrants, Nicola and Antoinette Iacocca, in 1924, Iacocca's given name was Lido, which he later changed to Lee. No one bought into the American Dream more than Lee's parents. On the strength of only a fourth-grade education, Nicola Iacocca opened a hot dog stand in Allentown, Pennsylvania, sold real estate, and established his own rental car business. He instilled his tireless work ethic in his son, who at age ten launched his own business career by waiting outside the local grocery store to cart home shoppers' groceries for a modest fee. This entrepreneurial spirit would never wane.

When the depression tore into the lives of millions of Americans, Lee's family fell on hard times. Although his parents' unflagging strength helped the family survive that nightmarish time, Lee vowed that never again would he let himself feel powerless, unable to control his own destiny. The depression also developed in him a strong distaste for waste of any kind, leading him to search constantly for the most efficient way to operate. Perhaps more important, he learned the lesson that hardship can strike at any moment. From then on, he vowed to keep himself prepared for any eventuality.

Though he wanted to fight for his country in World War II, complications resulting from a childhood bout with rheumatic fever prevented him from enlisting. Seeing higher education as the best alternative, he enrolled at Lehigh University to study business. His undergraduate performance earned him a Wallace Memorial Fellowship to Princeton, from which he graduated in 1946 with a Master's degree. Armed with the formal education to complement his intrinsic savvy and rock-solid principles, he took a job with the Ford Motor Company.

An early sign of Iacocca's visionary ability came during his tenure as a sales manager at Ford. With his district lagging behind all others in sales, he resolved to do something radically different. He devised a program called "56 for 56," offering brand-new 1956 Fords for 20 percent down and $56 a month over three years. A reasonable deal for the consumer, and a profitable one for the company, "56 for 56" was a resounding success. In no time, the young sales manager propelled his district from last place to first.

Iacocca then headed the Fairlane Committee, a group responsible for gathering and analyzing research to determine what types of cars to manufacture and market. The committee's research showed that the number of two-car families in American would increase dramatically in the 1960s. In response, Iacocca transformed the field of market research by coupling this data with social, psychological and motivational analyses, which revealed that Ford should develop an affordable, sporty, small vehicle to fill a nationally emerging sense of playfulness and adventure. The result was the 1964 Mustang, one of the most popular cars ever produced, and the catalyst for the rebirth of a declining automotive giant.

These successes earned Iacocca recognition as a seer of the industry and, in 1970, despite chairman Henry Ford II's reservations, he was appointed president of the company. While he oversaw a period of remarkable growth and profitability, his vision for Ford and that of its chairman increasingly diverged. Ultimately, the conflict between the two led to a widely publicized brouhaha culminating in Ford firing Iacocca.

As one of the messiest corporate divorces in modern history ensued, Iacocca used the notoriety created by the turmoil to put forward both a critique of Ford and a plan for overhauling the automobile industry. Iacocca had anticipated the crisis and had a master's grasp of how to take a potentially disastrous situation and transform it into an opportunity—a talent that did not go unnoticed by the deeply endangered Chrysler Corporation. Recognizing Iacocca's ability to anticipate change and transform disaster into opportunity, Chrysler's board of directors offered him chairmanship of the company—along with almost unparalleled power to reverse the organization's fortunes.

Iacocca stepped into the role knowing that he could not conduct business as usual—nothing short of massive change would bring the desired results. Gross mismanagement and massive debts plagued Chrysler to an even greater extent than Iacocca had feared. Knowing a shutdown could prove ruinous for the company—and the country—he requested that the U.S. government guarantee the company's outstanding loans. This unprecedented maneuver naturally prompted great opposition. However, Iacocca had correctly defined an issue far too important for the government to ignore. He made the request palatable by simply stating, "We at Chrysler borrow money the old-fashioned way. We pay it back." When the government accepted his brazen but brilliant proposal, the company's creditors felt secure in the knowledge that their loans would be honored, and Chrysler gained the breathing room it needed.

Buoyed by this initial victory, Iacocca dove into the next phase of his plan—trimming the fat from the company's operations in order to create the profits needed to get Chrysler back on sound financial footing. It turned into a corporate-wide rebuilding project of mammoth proportions. The company swiftly laid off unproductive and overpaid executives, closed inefficient factories, streamlined operations, and reduced its labor force—with each and every move carefully calculated to save money without damaging the organization's effectiveness. Chrysler rebounded dramatically from its woeful performance in the late seventies to increase its profitability and repay its debts by the early eighties. Iacocca had anticipated the need for change and executed the necessary drastic alterations with astounding success.

Lee Iacocca's unconventional methods earned him icon status. He wrote *Iacocca: An Autobiography* (Bantam, 1986),which sold two million copies, with all profits going to the American Diabetes Association in memory of his late wife. The Democratic Party even looked to him as a possible presidential candidate. But Iacocca only wanted to do what he had always done: seek new ways to solve old problems. So, he maintained his focus on keeping Chrysler on the cutting edge, devoting his free time to his family and several philanthropic organizations.

Lee Iacocca offers living proof that anticipating and responding to change with immediate, but careful and measured action can make things go right. Time after time, he tackled the same problems that baffled the rest of his industry, only to devise a solution that exceeded all expectations. He did it with common sense, determination and, above all, the ability to direct change. If those who ignore history are doomed to repeat it, those who ignore the future are destined to failure.

♣ Change and The New Murphy's Law

The winds of change can alarm us or excite us. Whatever our reaction, change will come about as certainly as death and taxes. Each of us must therefore learn to manage life's changes. Whether sudden or slow, unexpected or planned, they—and our reactions to them—will greatly determine whether we make things go right or allow happenstance or chaos to make them go wrong. The following essential lessons for managing change in our lives can help ensure that things go right:

- ♣ **Lesson 1: Never Give in to Circumstance.** Andy Grove did not permit the threat of death to immobilize him. When a situation appears to be beyond your control, do you ever give in or give up? Or do you search for aspects of the situation that you can master? When you encounter change, does the turn of events force you off your chosen path, or do you discipline yourself to incorporate it into your life in a positive way? Success depends on your ability to discover the opportunities to learn and grow embedded in any problem.

- ♣ **Lesson 2: When You Reach a Dead End, Look for the Detour Sign.** When Ludwig van Beethoven went deaf, he began listening to the music inside his own head. Do unanticipated changes in your life depress you, or do you look for ways around them? Does a nasty surprise tempt you to quit your course? When change surprises you with what looks like a brick wall, look for the window of opportunity in that wall.

♣ **Lesson 3: Look Beyond Yourself.** Robert Landau put his own needs behind those of others more needy than himself. Does a downward shift in your own fortunes propel you to self-pity, or do you put your own situation in perspective? Reaching out to help others less fortunate than yourself can provide the best antidote to self-pity and brooding over whatever fate has handed you.

♣ **Lesson 4: Change Yourself Before It's Too Late.** Like Albert Schweitzer, you can initiate change in your life. Has your career ever begun to feel like an old habit you can't change? Do you ever pause to wonder what greater success you might achieve if you tried a dramatically different path than the one you have been traveling? It's never too late to revisit your dreams and, if you feel you've lost them, to recapture their invigorating power.

♣ **Lesson 5: Act Boldly.** Had Lee Iacocca tried to institute only small, gradual changes, his company may have run out of time and financing. When you perceive that you should engineer a drastic change in your life or career, do you just think about it, or do you act on it decisively? Have you ever turned your back on necessary change simply because you feared the consequences of rocking the boat? Boldness will seldom harm you as much as passivity and inaction.

True, you cannot always fully control your own destiny. Sometimes you can chart your own path; at other times, however, the winds of change may blow you off your expected course. Your chances for a successful and happy life depend on learning to welcome change, to invite it, and to use it to make things go right.

Rule 4

Gain Power by Giving It Away

"Our power is not so much in us as through us."

Harry Emerson Fosdick

♣ THE PATH TO VICTORY

The history of our country has been written with the blood of men and women who sacrificed their lives in a continuing struggle to replace self-serving autocratic control with freedom and democratic rule. The same holds true for our corporations, where the old model of all-powerful bosses ordering people around has given way to a more empowering environment of flatter hierarchies and self-directed teams.

No one likes a bully. Anyone who acts as a tyrant attracts only ill-will and bitterness from others, and often loses power when those below him or her team up and rebel against the tyranny. Wise people, however, whether they work in the political, social, or business realm, have long known that the surest way to *achieve* and *maintain* power involves bestowing it on others, who invariably rise to the occasion and make things go right for themselves and their organizations. Those who delegate authority—treating people around them with trust and respect—engender goodwill, and with each morsel of power they give to others, they find more trust and influence returning to them. Such people become magnets for power. Coach Mike Krzyzewski (Coach K) provides just such a magnet for Duke University's Blue Devils basketball team.

Imagine playing in the final round of the NCAA basketball tournament. You are a point guard on Coach K's Blue Devils squad, and you take an in-bounds pass with twenty seconds remaining on the clock. You need to score two points to tie the game, three points to win. Your center stands near the three-point line, wildly signaling to you that he is open, but you think that you could race down court and tie or win the game yourself. What do you choose to do? Do you keep the ball or pass it? Do you risk trying for a long-shot three-point basket yourself? Or do you enable your teammate to score? If you're a Duke Blue Devil, no doubt would cross your mind: you would do what's best for the team, even if it means that you won't be the one whose game-saving shot gets replayed on the evening news.

Coach K says that he acquired much of his coaching philosophy while serving as a captain in the United States Army: "Being an officer was good training for coaching, and vice versa. It forces you to mold a group of men with a variety of backgrounds into a cohesive unit." Coach K never settles for producing one or two star players backed up by a crowd of "extras," but strives always to build a well-rounded team. He considers his mission as a coach "to motivate each player in such a way that he performs at his best while helping the team perform at its best."

Coach K does not just impose his ideas about shared responsibility and shared glory on his players. True to his own words, Coach K himself recognizes situations in which the team will benefit more when his players advise each other than when he dictates or lectures to them. He remains willing to make the most of his team members' various strengths. "Brian Davis was an excellent communicator," he said of one player. So, rather than going out himself to offer input to other players, "I would sometimes have him talk directly to an individual on the floor."

At half-time Coach K employs another strategy to empower his team. During the fifteen-minute break, he addresses his team briefly to settle their nerves and encourage or challenge them as the situation requires, then he and his staff retire to another room to review the first half of the game and discuss changes in strategy. Coach K believes that this break from the coach's presence empowers his players: "They can rest and talk amongst themselves about their performance. Sometimes, without the coaches present, one of the players will make a comment to another player or the rest of the team that is more effective than anything I say all night."

Since taking charge of the Blue Devils in 1980, Coach K has molded the team into an enduring national powerhouse. As Tom Emma, a former Duke player, explains, "He always does the right thing for his players, not only when it comes to basketball, but in every aspect of life." By showing respect for his team members' opinions and ideas about the course the team should take, Coach K has inspired many of his players to believe in their own abilities more than ever before. The confidence he has instilled in his players accounts for the extraordinary academic success of the Blue

Devils' squad members: all but two students who played in the last four seasons have graduated on time—an unprecedented record.

In recognition of his ability to inspire his players both on and off the court, Duke University recently honored Coach K with the University Medal for Distinguished Meritorious Service. His refreshing outlook has also earned him recognition and admiration on a national level; *Sporting News* has offered the praise that Coach K "is what is right about sports."

As Mike Krzyzewski so aptly demonstrates, those who hope to make things go right for themselves often start by helping others to make things go right. Think of power as a commodity, like money, that you can either bury in the backyard or invest in the stock market. If you hoard it, your power can only lie dormant. If you wisely invest it in others, it will accrue interest and dividends. This model of investment can be applied to four spheres of power in our lives:

THE FOUR SPHERES OF POWER

1 The Global Village

2 Society's Grass Roots

3 The Cooperative Organization

4 The Unified Team

What would you do if you witnessed inequity and injustice that affected millions? Would you turn your head and ignore the problem? Or would you remember the adage that "there is strength in numbers," and recruit others to help right the wrong?

Have you ever encountered an ineffective or weak law that perpetuates a dangerous situation for the community? Would you consider starting a grassroots movement to amend the law?

What would you do if you found yourself in charge of a large organization? If many people were looking to you to guide them to success, would you try to hold onto all of the decision-making power, or would you involve the entire group in the process?

How can you forge a team out of a group of individuals with little in common? If a potential team member has felt powerless all of his or her life, how can you empower that person?

Let's meet four individuals who effectively invested power in others and earned great returns on their investments when addressing these different spheres of influence.

❧ THE GLOBAL VILLAGE

On August 15, 1947, the British freed India from colonial rule, an event that brought to a successful conclusion Mohandas Gandhi's final non-violent revolutionary campaign, "Quit India." Gandhi achieved a major breakthrough in the revolutionary process of human history through his unbending policy of non-violence and through sharing power with millions of Indians. Although he began his revolution in relative obscurity and with little influence, as Gandhi began to share the little power he did possess with others, he found that his own sphere of influence and the effectiveness of his political cause expanded exponentially.

Mohandas Karamchand Gandhi was born to a prominent family in the western state of Porbandar, India, on October 2, 1869. Growing up, he learned that to get ahead in life one must cooperate with the English and conform to their system. To be perceived as well-educated and prominent, one must not only speak English without an Indian accent, but also wear

London-made clothing. Thus, Gandhi's father, a state prime minister, often dressed in Western clothing when conducting business, although he greatly disliked it. "If I were a painter," Gandhi later wrote, "I could paint my father's disgust and the torture on his face as he was putting his legs in his stockings and feet into ill-fitting and uncomfortable boots." But Gandhi's father felt powerless to dress otherwise.

When Gandhi was still a young boy, the family moved from the city of Porbandar to the town of Rajkot, in the northwest of India. Gandhi's father held a more important position there, but the family's new living conditions were deplorable. In Rajkot, only the British could occupy the fine houses in the best section of town. No matter their position or wealth, Indians had no choice but to live in what the English called the "native town," a crowded, dirty and noisy slum with dirt roads and no sewer system. The British section, on the other hand, sported paved roads, sanitary facilities and modern conveniences, all funded by taxes levied on Indian residents which never found their way to the "native town." This first experience with mandated segregation made a lasting impression on the young Mohandas Gandhi.

At age seventeen, Gandhi enrolled in an Indian college. Knowing, however, that the colonial powers would never respect a degree from an Indian institution, the young scholar convinced his upwardly mobile family to send him to London to study law. When he arrived in London in 1888, Mohandas Gandhi maintained English habits and dress, just as his father had often done. He was learning to "play the English gentleman," he said later. With his top hat, fine suit, silk shirt, spats, and silver-topped cane, he looked every bit the well-heeled young lawyer.

Upon graduation, Gandhi returned to India to practice law, but he made little impact in the profession.

Therefore, he soon accepted a job in South Africa with an Indian firm operating there. It was in that country that Gandhi's social conscience, first ignited in the ghettoes of Rajkot, became inflamed. Disgusted that his fellow countrymen in South Africa were treated more poorly than animals, Gandhi dedicated himself to their struggle for basic political and social rights.

Gandhi himself encountered terrible prejudice in South Africa. In that country, he explained, "I discovered that as a man and as an Indian I had no rights." Once, taking the train from Durban to Pretoria, with the appropriate first-class ticket, he suffered painful humiliation when the authorities physically threw him out of the first-class compartment. Even in the coach section he was unwelcome, as the conductor abused him verbally and physically when he firmly refused to move to an inferior seat.

Gandhi resolved that no self-respecting human being should be forced to endure such injustice but, instead of just moving back to his homeland, he chose to fight for the welfare of his fellow Indians in South Africa. Soon, his focus shifted from getting ahead as a lawyer to making things go right for all non-whites in his adopted country. There, in May of 1894, he founded the Natal Indian Congress with some of his Indian friends and began the fight to improve sanitation, education and housing conditions for his people. For twenty years, he funded his activism in South Africa through his law practice.

In 1906, during a period of particularly tense relations between Indians and Europeans in the South African Transvaal region, Gandhi first formulated his own theory of passive resistance and strength in numbers: *satyagraha*. Gandhi defined satyagraha as a "soul-force pure and simple." He explained that this political stance differed from the usual theory of passive resistance: "If we... let others believe that we are weak and helpless and therefore offer passive resistance, our resistance will never make us strong.... On the other hand, if we are satyagrahis and offer satyagraha believing ourselves to be strong, two clear consequences result from it. Fostering the idea of strength, we grow stronger and stronger every day. With the increase in our strength, our satyagraha, too, becomes more effective...." In other words, Gandhi viewed peaceful protest not as a passive act, but as an active means through which he and his fellow Indians could demonstrate and magnify their political power. To Gandhi, each individual present at a protest, not just the leader, delivered an unconquerable message, with every soul adding the same amount of energy to the soul-force of satyagraha.

When a new series of "Black Acts" in the early 1900s proposed to restrict even further the rights of non-whites, Gandhi organized a vast march in protest. In 1913, he and 2,000 other Indians set off on foot to cross the Transvaal region, an area largely restricted to them. Though harassed and abused by South African troops, the marchers maintained their dedication to non-violence, reacting always and only with dignity and patience. The restraint and courtesy shown by this band of ragged protesters under intense provocation won such worldwide admiration that intense international pressure ultimately forced the South African government to reconsider the anti-Indian acts. Gandhi had empowered his thousands of followers, many of whom were destitute coolie laborers who had never before considered themselves of any significance. The strength generated by this motley assemblage, however, changed the policies of a nation.

With his first big campaign a success, Gandhi headed home to India in order to involve himself in the movement for *swaraj*, or self-rule. Gandhi hoped to apply his theory of satyagraha to the self-rule movement, furthering the cause through the irresistible power of the soul-force. He began, on a small scale, to recruit Indians into his movement through working to improve conditions for the lower classes in his homeland. First he organized a peaceful protest against the plight of peasants in the Champaran region who toiled endlessly for miserable wages in the indigo-growing industry, an industry rigidly controlled by the colonial government. "Satyagraha brought this age-long abuse to an end in a few months," Gandhi proudly stated.

He then moved on to represent the oppressed peasantry in other provinces. On more than one occasion, he was attacked, both physically and politically, by the government, but he unwaveringly responded with the strength and patience derived from his own convictions and from his millions of followers in the satyagraha movement. Finally, in 1947, forty years after Mohandas Gandhi had formulated the theory behind it, the Indian fight for independence triumphed as Britain pulled out of what had been one of its most lucrative colonies.

At a surprisingly early age, Mohandas Gandhi realized that he could not attain happiness climbing the ladder of power within the colonial system. Personal wealth and success would mean little when all around him his countrymen suffered horrible deprivation. He knew that when he stopped playing by the rules of what he called the "subtle but effective system of terrorism" implemented by the British, he gave up all chance of advancing in that system. He would never achieve the power that wealth can bring, but through his satyagraha movement he achieved much more.

Gandhi's admiring and grateful countrymen gave him the title Mahatma, "Great Soul," an apt title for a man who eschewed personal power to invest it in others. Things went right for millions of souls because he knew how to gain power by giving it away.

♣ Society's Grass Roots

John Walsh, the well-known host of the *America's Most Wanted* television series, has also made his mark by empowering others. In the face of the most personally devastating circumstance, Walsh managed to transform his own grief and rage into a positive social force.

Although a well-known and recognizable celebrity today, John Walsh never planned on a career in television. In fact, in 1981, his whole life revolved around his family and the hotel management company he co-owned in Hollywood, Florida. The business was doing quite well, and his personal life seemed to be going along smoothly, too, centering on his wife, Reve, and their six-year-old son, Adam.

Suddenly, however, on July 27, 1981, the Walshes' universe collapsed when Adam disappeared on a shopping trip with his mother. The Walshes immediately called the police, but when the police proved skeptical, the terrified parents were compelled to search for their son on their own. Faced with the horrifying possibility that his son had been abducted, John Walsh could not believe that the police possessed no effective means for spreading word about the missing boy even to his neighborhood, let alone to the general public.

The ineffectiveness of the existing system astounded and shocked the desperate father. When a child's life hung in the balance, he thought, shouldn't the authorities pursue every possible avenue of inquiry? Someone out there might have seen something; someone might be staring at his boy in a restaurant, an arcade, or a mall, completely unaware that anything was amiss. John Walsh barraged the police with questions about the course of their investigation into his son's disappearance. Receiving no satisfactory response, however, he quickly realized that he could not afford to waste any time trying to prod the unresponsive system into motion. Instead, he brought his business acumen to bear on the problem, devising the best possible means to find his son without the police department's help.

Walsh understood at the outset that he could never achieve this goal on his own. Thus, he drew up and posted flyers with Adam's picture and description in his neighborhood and beyond, hoping that someone would recognize the boy. Next, he solicited the local media to cover the story of his missing son. The media expressed reluctance air such a "depressing" story, but eventually they gave in to Walsh's persistence, broadcasting, for the first time, the picture of a missing child over the local airways.

John Walsh didn't stop there. He knew that a kidnapper could have easily transported his son out of the local area, so he lobbied the national media as well, to air news of his son's disappearance. Despite the great emotional toll he knew it would exact on him and his wife, he even agreed to accept bookings on nationally televised talk shows, hoping desperately that someone would see their son's photo, recognize him, and pick up the phone.

Tragically, just as John and Reve Walsh were preparing to appear on one of these talk shows with a group of other parents of missing children, John received word that a young boy's skull had been found, and that the police had tentatively identified it as Adam's. Walsh debated whether or not to share the news with Reve; he finally decided not to do so since the skull could turn out not to be their son's. He also debated whether or not to go on with the talk show appearance that day. Again, since Adam might still be alive somewhere, he decided to continue, hoping for the best for as long as he could.

The Walshes made their appearance; during the telecast, Adam's picture and those of the other missing children aired on national television. For the first time ever, a national grassroots effort to help find a missing child had galvanized the entire country. After the show, Reve went to a restaurant with the other parents to talk about further steps they could take to recover their children. John returned to the hotel room alone, where, before long, he received the phone call he had dreaded. The police confirmed that the remains they had located were, indeed, Adam's.

When Walsh hung up the phone, his rage at the unspeakable fate that had befallen his young son overwhelmed him. He broke everything in the room that he could get his hands on, overturned furniture and pounded his fist into the wall, all the while crying and screaming out his anguish. Though it seemed to him that he could never recover his senses, John Walsh also knew that he could not continue his tormented frenzy. Reve had yet to learn of her son's fate. Walsh composed himself as best he could, then phoned the restaurant where Reve was still planning how best to recover her now forever lost son. He asked Reve to return to the hotel so that he could give her the news in private.

John and Reve Walsh grieved terribly for Adam, blaming themselves for not having safeguarded him, the police for their clumsy handling of the case, the media for their reluctance to air a story on a missing child and, most of all, of course, the faceless animal, still at large, who had stolen their son from them. Despite their mountain of grief and grievances, the Walshes did not allow much time to pass before continuing for others the crusade they had started for their son. Might they not ease their own pain by fixing the cracks in the system that had failed them in their efforts to save Adam?

John and Reve saw the need for new legislation designed to assist parents and officials in their search for a missing child. Comprehending the legislative nightmares involved in pushing a bill through Congress, the Walshes nevertheless felt that the tremendous effort could reap huge dividends. If they could put into place an effective means of publicizing the case of one missing child, and thereby retrieve that child, Adam would not have died in vain.

The Walshes reluctantly relocated, temporarily, to Washington in order to fight full-time for their cause, reaching out to hundreds of thousands of people, one small group at a time. John Walsh launched a grassroots campaign, speaking to virtually anyone who would listen, from groups of ten or twelve parents who had also lost children to a gathering of hundreds of Congressional representatives. He established such a tremendous following, receiving tens of thousands of letters of support from around the country, that Congress began to see the folly of ignoring the demands of a man who had received a mandate from millions. Ultimately, the work of the Walshes and their supporters led to the passage of the Missing Children Act of 1982 and the Missing Children's Assistance Act of 1984, which founded the National Center for Missing and Exploited Children. In their son's memory, the Walshes also set up the Adam Walsh Child Resource Center, a non-profit organization dedicated to continuing the legislative reform that the pair had so effectively begun.

In 1988, seven years after Adam's death, the Fox television network approached John Walsh to host *America's Most Wanted*, a new show that would put the faces of wanted criminals on the screen in the hope that the public could help capture them. At first, Walsh felt reluctant to accept the offer, because it would mean limiting his work lobbying Congress on behalf of a variety of victims' rights groups. He also worried that becoming a "TV personality" would harm his credibility in Washington. Would government

70

THE NEW MURPHY'S LAW

officials still take him seriously? Intrigued by the concept of the show, however, John Walsh agreed to introduce the first episode, although he would not commit to the role of permanent host for the series.

When he arrived to tape his introduction, producers of *America's Most Wanted* asked Walsh if he would like to see the first crime re-creation they had taped. While watching the criminal history of escaped murderer David James Roberts, who had been serving six life sentences for murder, Walsh learned that two of Roberts' victims had been less than two years old. Appalled that this animal was still roaming the streets, a danger to children and adults everywhere, Walsh saw what he must do to make things go right. "I couldn't believe it. 'I'm the father of a murdered child, and here's a guy who killed two kids,' I said. 'Wouldn't it be great if we caught this guy? Wouldn't that be something? I'm going to talk to my wife about this.'"

When Reve saw John's enthusiasm for the show's possibilities, she immediately encouraged him to take the job as host. John, however, proposed a few stipulations before he would finally accept. He wanted to make certain that information gleaned from the airing of the show would not benefit just federal law enforcement, but local and state police as well. After all, he had witnessed firsthand the problems caused by the lack of coordination between different law enforcement agencies. In addition, he said he wanted everyone in the nation to be able to provide any information they had via a toll-free 800 number. The network accepted Walsh's demands, and *America's Most Wanted* first aired on Sunday, February 7, 1988. In the ten years since, the show has assisted in the capture of more than 400 of America's most dangerous criminals.

Today, Walsh continues to act as an outspoken advocate for children's rights, and for victims' rights in general, even as he continues to host *America's Most*

Wanted. He has empowered victims of violent crime through improved legislation and law enforcement cooperation, and he has empowered the viewing public by allowing each individual to participate in the investigative process. By helping to give others more power to protect themselves, John Walsh has earned the respect and trust of millions. He has been honored for his work by three presidents, numerous law enforcement agencies, and by the media, including *CBS Portraits*, which named him one of the "100 Americans Who Changed History." The many victims and potential victims who benefit from the legislation he has passed—and all of us who feel a little bit safer because he has helped remove so many criminals from our streets—owe a debt of thanks to this man who understood how to mobilize the power of a national grassroots movement by empowering others with the knowledge they needed to take action themselves.

♣ THE COOPERATIVE ORGANIZATION

In the early 1980s, Jack Welch assumed leadership of General Electric, a company as legendary for pioneering management techniques as for pioneering technology. GE's tradition of innovative management included new techniques such as strategic planning and management by objectives. However, by the time Welch took the helm, the industry giant had grown so complacent that it risked entering a downward spiral. As the new CEO, Welch set about immediately to reenergize the company.

From the outset of his tenure, Welch knew he must move decisively. Initially, he believed a top down surgical approach involving massive downsizing and restructuring was the answer. This tactic soon garnered him the nickname "Neutron Jack": the leader who eliminates the people but leaves the buildings standing. Welch soon realized that he was removing people whose advice he sorely needed and whose efforts would be the key to powering up the declining giant. This realization led to one of the most dramatic leadership transformations in modern industry, vaulting Welch to the top rank of the world's CEOs and showing him to be a master practitioner of accruing power by giving it away.

With no clear sense of direction, the employees of GE had begun to expend their energy in ways that destabilized the organization. At the same time, they resisted change and depended on the accomplishments of the past. Welch, recognizing that the company's heritage and past accomplishments could not guarantee its future, faced considerable resistance to his change initiatives. A backlog of orders on such big-ticket items as steam locomotives, steam turbines, and nuclear power plants had lulled many GE executives into a false sense of security. For the moment they could overlook the fact that the company's profits depended on aging businesses that were growing slowly or not at all. Of GE's many operating units, only a few held solid market positions and some markets in which GE had traditionally done well, such as lighting, were beginning to decline.

To remedy the situation, Welch developed a new corporate vision to address the prospects of declining profits and reduced market share, setting the clear objective that each GE division must become either number one or two in its market or get out of that line of business. This required each GE worker to recommit to the welfare of the whole organization by examining all individual and team efforts to determine exactly *how* work was performed, and *why*. To engage everyone at GE in examining the company's effectiveness, Welch initiated a radical new strategy for evaluating corporate policies and procedures, which businesspeople worldwide have just recently begun to comprehend.

Inspired by the accuracy of GE's world-class medical imaging technology in evaluating the soundness of a person's health, Welch set out to involve all GE employees in the process of creating a "body scan" of their organization. To this end, he gathered a talented team of managers, researchers, and programmers to develop a brand-new tool for systems-wide performance assessment. This new system enabled each employee to produce a "Work Image," a summary of activities portraying his or her day-to-day work. The activity summary created by each person, combined with others' summaries, formed a picture of the operations of the organization as a whole. By revealing how people *really* spent their time, the Work Images provided a picture of where the company was actually allocating its resources.

Through Work Imaging, Jack Welch engaged each employee in the corporation's survival. In the process, everyone began to appreciate how individual activities influenced the overall health of the organization. Employees also got a clear sense of what they and their departments were doing right, and where they needed improvement. With this new tool, GE workers could finally measure and take responsibility for their own contributions as they worked to accomplish the company's new mission. Rather than receiving a mandate from the top to improve operations and focus energy on the mission, everyone at GE was asked to view his or her own Work Image and think concretely about how to improve performance. By giving this power to his employees, Welch demonstrated his understanding of the critical role that measurement and empowerment play in building a CEO's credibility and in overcoming fear of change.

Under Jack Welch's guidance, GE has sustained tremendous growth. It is now the most valuable company in the world, with a market capitalization of $254 billion. It has overcome Coca-Cola as America's greatest wealth creator. And GE stock rose in value by nearly 50 percent in one year alone—approximately the same growth achieved by Microsoft, but accomplished by a much bigger, 107-year-old company. Welch has said that sustaining this success depends on continuing to improve GE's empowering management approaches.

As part of his plan to encourage his team members to work to their fullest potential, Welch has designed a bonus program directly tied to the success of product and service quality initiatives. He continues to institute new and innovative leadership programs to involve all employees in streamlining and improving GE's corporate operations. "Control your own destiny, or someone else will," he advises the members of his organization. In every way, "Neutron Jack" has evolved into an inspirational leader who involves his team in all aspects of the organization's, and their own, survival. By giving power away, he enables each GE employee to make things go right.

♣ THE UNIFIED TEAM

Sometimes empowering others simply means giving people a sense of their own power—and the feeling of entitlement necessary to claim it. As spotlighted in the movie *Stand and Deliver*, Jaime Escalante, a Los Angeles schoolteacher, made it his mission to mine the talents of a group of students whom society, their school, and even themselves had written off as failures.

Escalante taught for fourteen years in Bolivia before deciding to migrate to the United States in 1964, at age thirty-four. He arrived first in Puerto Rico, where he studied science and math, then moved to California, where he initially felt lost because he lacked both fluency in English and necessary teaching credentials. Escalante could have given up at that point and gone home, but already he felt a great commitment to and admiration for his newly chosen home. In America, he thought, where everyone is equal, he stood as much of a chance to succeed as anyone else. With great dedication, he worked days as a busboy and cook while studying at night for an electronics degree. Once he earned that degree, he worked as an electronics factory technician and spent his nights pursuing a math degree.

Finally, at age forty-four, the tireless Escalante took a job teaching mathematics at Garfield High in East Los Angeles, which served one of the toughest, most crime-ridden districts in the state. Every day, drugs, gangs and violence plagued the school and its students. On his first day there, Escalante faced a classroom of teen-agers that school officials considered "unteachable," and worse. Escalante immediately made it clear to these kids that he did not buy into that label; then he went to work showing his students that just because they faced a tougher challenge than most, they need not resign themselves to a dead-end life in the ghetto. Escalante knew that most of his students came from families who had lived in poverty for so many generations that they felt powerless to improve their condition in life. He impressed upon them the futility of this insidious complacency, driving home the power of a good education and the pride that comes from achieving a goal against great odds.

Whereas these words might normally have seemed like a lot of hot air, coming from a teacher who had experienced a similar struggle, they carried a lot of weight. The possibilities he described were news to them, as was Escalante's strong faith in their potential.

Amazingly, at a school in danger of losing its accreditation, Escalante managed to motivate his students to study calculus devotedly and even come to school on Saturdays to prepare to take the Advanced Placement (AP) Calculus Test.

By providing examples of how mathematics worked in their daily lives, and through the strength of his own character and dedication, Escalante inspired his students with a newfound confidence in their capacity to learn, and in the value of a good education. The AP Calculus Test for which Escalante's students were preparing during the 1981-82 school year was so difficult that nationwide only two percent of the students who took it managed to pass. Escalante's Garfield High students, the first group from their school ever to attempt the test, all passed with flying colors. The Educational Testing Service, however, noting the unprecedented success of the students and that several students had made the same mistakes, invalidated the scores upon the suspicion that they had cheated.

This setback broke Escalante's heart, not to mention those of the students who had worked so hard and against such odds—but he refused to let it destroy his students' newfound sense of power. He and the students challenged the ETS, which let them take the exam again, this time under armed guard—and, again, most of the students passed with high scores. Escalante became a national hero of education as subsequent classes of Garfield High students studied for and passed the exam. Eighteen students from Escalante's class attempted the AP Calculus Test in 1982, and those who passed accounted for fully one-third of Hispanic students who did so nationwide. By 1991, 570 Garfield High students were taking AP exams in math and other subjects.

Escalante went on to create a television series with the Foundation for Advancements in Science and Education, called *FUTURES… with Jaime Escalante*. The series, which brings mathematics to life by showing students its applications from skateboarding to space shuttles, won a Peabody Award for excellence. Eventually, after twenty years of teaching, Escalante received the United States Presidential Medal in honor of his outstanding achievements, and in 1988 he provided the basis for the main character in the acclaimed movie *Stand and Deliver*. Escalante shows his students, and us, too, that race, history and class need never stand in the way of achievement. He gave his students more than an understanding of calculus; he gave them the power to make things go right.

 POWER AND THE NEW MURPHY'S LAW

An individual can easily feel insignificant when he or she is but one of hundreds in a company, thousands in a nation, or millions in the world. However, as the individuals in this chapter illustrate, one empowered person can make a big difference. Both the one who gives power away and the one who receives power benefit from the act. To win the same benefits, you can incorporate these lessons into your own life:

♣ **Lesson 1: Restrain Selfishness**. Coach K teaches his players the value of setting aside personal glory for the success of the team. When you find yourself in a position of power within a team, do you tap the abilities of each individual? Do you enjoy seeing others succeed as a result of providing them with guidance and assistance? Whenever selfishness tempts you to behave in a controlling or manipulative way, remember that your own success depends on the success of those around you.

♣ **Lesson 2: Never Let the Resistance of Others Rob You of Power**. Gandhi and his "soul-force" encountered much resistance before achieving their goal of independence for India. Are you able to sustain your dedication to an important goal even when you encounter a lot of discouragement? Does the opposition of others ever cause you to abandon your goal? Do you routinely mobilize the support of others to overcome opposition? Can you inspire those around you to do the same? Define every obstacle, roadblock or detour as an opportunity for greater empowerment.

♣ **Lesson 3: Rely on the Strength of Many.** More than 400 felons sit behind bars because John Walsh empowered honest people to identify the dishonest in their midst. Do you ever feel alone and powerless when something goes wrong in your life or work? When you set a goal that you know you cannot reach alone, do you share the information others need to enlist in your cause? When accomplishing a goal requires many hands, do whatever it takes to let the power flow to those hands.

♣ **Lesson 4: Employ Strengths While Improving Weaknesses**. As Jack Welch's story illustrates, if you help people recognize and appreciate their various strengths and weaknesses, you stand a much better chance of achieving your goal. Do you ever feel exasperated over someone's weakness or jealous of someone's strength? When you encounter weaknesses in others do you let those weaknesses define that person, or do you look for strengths that might help them overcome those weaknesses? Try to recognize and measure the strengths and weaknesses in yourself and others, knowing that success derives not only from what you do well but from improving what you don't do well.

♣ **Lesson 5: Inspire Others to Empower Themselves.** Jaime Escalante taught more than math—he taught his students that they possessed the power to improve their own lives. Do you work or live with people who lack self-confidence? Can you think of a way to help them feel more confident and sure of themselves? By serving as a role model and by respecting the ability of others to use the power of their talents effectively, you can inspire those around you to accomplish more than they ever dreamed possible.

No one can accomplish much alone, but when many people band together in a common cause, each enjoying the power to make things happen, the right thing usually happens. The people in this chapter have altered the courses of teams, companies, communities, and even countries. By giving power away, they gained the power to make things go right.

Rule 5

Practice Strategic Humility

"An open mind collects more riches than an open purse."

Will Henry

♣ CHUNKY MONKEY BUSINESS

When competent, strong-willed people recognize that they don't have all the knowledge they need and then take action to do something about it, we call that an act of strategic humility. You know where you want to go (strategy), you admit that you don't know exactly how to get there (humility), so you ask for help (strategic humility). Admitting a lack of knowledge or expertise and seeking help to acquire it requires self-confidence, of course, and self-confidence can be hard to muster when we feel inadequate in a situation. But it always pays off, as the meteoric success of Ben & Jerry's ice cream company aptly illustrates.

Ben Cohen and Jerry Greenfield first met in seventh grade gym class. They quickly became close friends on the basis, as they put it, of their shared "deep and sincere appreciation of good food and lots of it." After high school, they initially set off on divergent paths, but always maintained a close friendship. Ben drove an ice cream truck for $100 a week and as much ice cream as he could eat, and Jerry enrolled in college to prepare for medical school. While Jerry studied chemistry, Ben went on to dabble in various jobs, ranging from Manhattan taxi driver to Pinkerton guard.

When Jerry graduated from college and couldn't get into medical school, the two friends put their heads together and thought about their futures. What sort of business would make them happy, they wondered. "We just wanted to do something that would be fun," Ben explains in their cookbook, *Ben & Jerry's Double Dip* Dip (Simon and Schuster, 1997),whose introduction describes the history of their business. "We wanted to be our own bosses and work exactly when, where, and how we wanted." True to their original interests, they came up with the idea to open a little restaurant and feature one of their favorite foods, either bagels or ice cream. When they compared the high cost of bagel-making equipment to ice-cream-making machines, they knew the answer. Ice cream it would be. Next, they picked their dream location: rural Vermont. There they set about learning the food business by opening a coffee shop in a little store in downtown Burlington. At the same time, they began studying up on the ice-cream business by enrolling in a correspondence course on ice-cream making offered through Pennsylvania State University.

By 1978, Ben and Jerry had pooled their resources, borrowed another $4,000 and, with a total investment of $12,000, renovated a rickety old gas station they'd found in Burlington, and started their business. They expected the venture to last a few years, until they found something else to do. They certainly didn't expect runaway success. And neither did anyone else—considering their unorthodox business practices. Ben and Jerry were determined to build their business around a concept of "linked prosperity" which ensured that all employees shared in the profits of the corporation from its very inception. Over and over again, experts told them, "Nobody's ever done that before. You'd be crazy to do that. It won't work." However, the maverick ice-cream makers stuck to their ideals.

As Ben & Jerry's grew, the owners remained true to their original principles. While they knew that their unconventional practices might limit their profits, they believed that customers would gladly pay a little more for a high-quality product if they respected the company's strong business ethics and commitment to social and environmental responsibility. Their unorthodox approach worked.

Ben and Jerry had vowed that they would remain the guiding force behind their business for as long as it existed. Their determination sprang from their belief that since business is the most powerful influence in modern society, businesses must accept responsibility for ensuring social and environmental well-being. Under their guidance, Ben & Jerry's would not only use environmentally sound manufacturing processes, such as recycling and composting, but also operate as a good neighbor, a respectful employer, and a supplier of top-quality products.

In 1995, after nearly two decades of success, Ben Cohen and Jerry Greenfield found themselves in a difficult situation. The consumer demand for their product was escalating so rapidly they could not keep up with it. With the company's skyrocketing sales, the partners did not feel that they could competently steer the company through this period of runaway growth.

Admitting that they could not continue to grow all by themselves, they decided to search for a compatible Chief Executive Officer to take over the reins from Ben.

Given their values-based business philosophy, Ben and Jerry did not want to hire the sort of buttoned-down, bottom-line-obsessed CEO most large companies prefer. A "million dollar man" would, they thought, put profit before principles. Instead, they wanted someone who would feel comfortable with their corporate philosophy, especially the idea of "linked prosperity," which mandated that Ben & Jerry's purchase supplies from small farms, because such farms greatly benefit society and the environment. The new CEO must not grimace at paying higher prices to these suppliers.

The new CEO must also honor Ben & Jerry's Human Resources policies—employee-focused policies that included annual evaluations by employees of their supervisors, training sessions to help employees understand both the purpose and process of these evaluations, and employee involvement in all key decisions made at the company, from benefits packages to the establishment of on-site day care facilities. Ben and Jerry decided they would compromise on only one issue: they would pay the right person more than seven times the pay received by the lowest-level employees, which had been their traditional salary cap.

In late 1995, after an extensive search, Ben Cohen announced the appointment of Robert Holland Jr., as the new company CEO. Holland's beliefs seemed consistent with those of the company's founders. He knew from the outset that his own success depended on maintaining the family-owned feeling of an increasingly large corporation, and so he brought a light touch to bear in his new role. Steering the company through its big growth stage with leadership and poise, he expanded Ben & Jerry's to many new international and domestic locations. He also introduced new products to the market, such as sorbets and non-fat frozen yogurts, and saw to it that Ben & Jerry's new production plant was running smoothly.

Ben and Jerry knew what they didn't know. Admitting that they lacked the know-how to manage the next phase of their company's growth, they sought help. By doing so, they proved the power of practicing strategic humility, one of the most difficult aspects of making things go right. As difficult as it may be, there are sound motivations for admitting to yourself that you don't know everything you need to know to succeed in your life and your work. In this chapter, we will explore four of these motivations:

FOUR MOTIVATIONS FOR HUMILITY

1. Creates Self-Esteem
2. Inspires the Respect of Others
3. Allows for Continuous Learning
4. Provides a Role Model

Examining these four motivations for strategic humility will allow you to better assess your capabilities, admit shortcomings, and seek necessary help.

Have you ever felt that you simply could not live up to your own self-image or that the image you have created for yourself does not match reality?

Do you feel that others respect you? Do you respect yourself? Do you desire self-respect and the respect of others?

At any point in your life and career have you felt that you knew it all? Have you ever come to a point where you felt that learning more about your profession was unnecessary or useless?

What role models guide your work and your life? Are you a role model? What knowledge or skill or achievement must you acquire to become a role model for others?

These and similar questions have led the people we will meet in this chapter to set aside their assumptions or misconceptions about their capabilities. They all knew, or thought they knew, where they wanted to go, but came to realize that they lacked the full means to get there and sought help. In other words, they practiced strategic humility in order to make things go right.

♣ CREATES SELF-ESTEEM

In 1927, at the age of fifteen, Chuck Jones dropped out of high school and enrolled in the Chouinard Art Institute (now the California Institute for the Arts) in Los Angeles. At Chouinard, he threw himself into learning everything he needed to know to become a great artist in the "classical" tradition. Not long after he began his first life-drawing class, however, he grew despondent over the superior skill of his fellow students. Tempted to drop out, but unsure what to do, Jones sought the advice of his beloved Uncle Lynn. "They're a bunch of da Vincis," Jones said of his classmates. His own skills at depicting life-like characters, he admitted, paled by comparison. It's no use, he told his uncle, "you can't make a racehorse out of a pig."

"Perhaps," agreed his uncle, "But you can make a very fast pig."

Jones laughed, but then he saw the truth in his uncle's words. Whatever his talents, he would not sharpen them if he gave up. So, he stuck it out, learning that while he would never turn into a "da Vinci," he could turn into something equally satisfying. After graduating from Chouinard, Jones went to work as an animation cell washer at Iwerks, one of the first animation studios. His drawing skills, it turned out, suited cartoon animation beautifully. He advanced to assistant animator before being fired, then rehired, then fired again (by the Iwerks secretary, whom he would later marry). After leaving Iwerks for good, Jones worked for Warner Brothers where, at age twenty-five, he directed his first animated cartoon, *The Night Watchmen*. During his tenure at Warner Brothers, Jones and his colleagues from "Termite Terrace" (the animators' bungalow on the Warner lot) introduced many fanciful and fun characters. Jones himself created Wile E. Coyote, the Road Runner, Pepe Le Pew, and Marvin the Martian, among others.

Jones also worked for Disney for a while, an experience that revealed a big difference between Disney's and Warner Brothers' approach to their art form. Walt Disney sought to create characters that imitated life, Jones later explained, while he and his fellow animators at Warner Brothers focused on appealing to the imagination.

Chuck Jones' three Oscars, along with the endurance of the characters he created, established him as a superior practitioner of his craft. Even though he has accomplished much, Jones takes a very humble view of his talents: "A small child once said to me, 'You don't draw Bugs Bunny, you draw pictures of Bugs Bunny.' That's a very profound observation because he thinks the characters are alive, which, as far as I am concerned, is true."

Jones continued his creative work after Warner Brothers Animation closed in 1962 and, in 1966, he produced the now-classic American Christmas special, *Dr. Seuss' How the Grinch Stole Christmas*. Recently, his *What's Opera Doc*, a film featuring Elmer Fudd and Bugs Bunny, was inducted into the Library of Congress' National Film Registry, an honor accorded to only 100 films to date. It was, in fact, the first animated film inducted into this registry of "the most culturally, historically or aesthetically significant films of our time."

Chuck Jones succeeded because he practiced strategic humility, recognizing his limitations but making the most of what skills he did possess. And, yes, he sought help when he lamented his plight to his uncle Lynn. By overcoming his self-doubts, he became, as he describes himself, "a pretty fast pig"—someone who can make things go right.

♣ INSPIRES THE RESPECT OF OTHERS

Franklin Delano Roosevelt was one of the most confident and, to all appearances, even arrogant leaders in American history. Known as the "happy warrior," he waded readily into any dilemma with the air of someone who believed he could solve a problem by the sheer force of his will, intellect and charm. But behind this public image, the real Roosevelt was a man who, due to his battle with polio, had developed a profound humility and a keen awareness of his need for others. While his illness left him physically battered, it also gave him critically important insight into what it took to be an effective leader.

As a result of his illness, Roosevelt learned to compensate for physical and other limitations. Because he lacked complete mobility, and the ability to be everywhere at once, he surrounded himself with what he called "personal listeners," people in key posts who could go out into the world and collect the information he needed to make the decisions that a world leader must make. He saw these listeners almost as physical extensions of himself—his eyes and ears and legs.

One of Roosevelt's key listeners was a childhood friend, Livingston W. Houston, who later became president of the Rensselaer Polytechnic Institute in Troy, New York, and a world-renowned scientist and humanitarian in his own right. During the period just preceding the Second World War, Livingston accepted the position of an undersecretary in the Department of the Navy where he served as Roosevelt's "personal listener." His responsibility was to help the president "keep his ear to the ground" in matters of defense. By listening carefully, Livingston helped to effect a major change in military tactics, which probably influenced the outcome of the war in the Pacific.

One day Livingston was lunching with a naval captain who appeared deeply distressed. "What's wrong?" Livingston asked him. The captain, with an air of despondence, outlined his grave concerns over the ability of America's warships to protect themselves in the event of an air attack. The Navy's policies were outdated, he said, but he could not get any of the Navy brass to listen to his concerns.

When Livingston Houston pressed for details, the captain described the several different stations on board each battleship and the rules, or "gunnery command policies," that governed how these stations would respond to an attack. These policies stated that each individual station on board each ship should choose their own targets.

"I don't see a problem with that strategy," Houston responded.

The Navy captain forged on, "These policies were set over 100 years ago! Today, a single airplane can carry enough ammunition to cause fatal damage to one of our warships, and these planes can reach speeds of up to 400 miles per hour in a dive! What if only *one* of the gunnery commanders on board a ship chooses to target an aircraft diving in at that speed because the others have independently decided to focus on float-ing targets, or more distant craft?"

Houston began to understand the captain's point. An airplane in a direct dive presents the smallest possible target, a tough mark to hit as it comes screaming toward you at 400 miles per hour. Obviously, the more shells aimed at such a target, the better the chances of hitting it, and of saving the ship under attack.

Houston asked one last question: "How do you propose to solve this problem, then?" The captain, relieved, and more than a little surprised that the undersecre-tary showed such an interest in his concerns, told Livingston that the solution lay in synchronizing all the gunnery posts under one command in the event of attack. In that way, firepower could be concentrated in sufficient force to give the ship a reasonable chance of destroying a plane zooming in from an almost ver-tical angle. In the event of an attack by more than one plane, firepower could be divided as equally as possi-ble to concentrate on both incoming craft. This would require central gunnery command, a major change in battleship protocol.

Livingston wondered aloud why the captain had not explained this problem to the Navy's admirals and the secretary of war. To this, the captain responded, "Well I've tried. I've tried for over six months to convince them! They say this flies in the face of tradition, and that if I don't shut up, I will be cashiered out of the Navy."

The undersecretary knew what to do—sidestep the Navy brass and take the matter directly to their boss: the Commander in Chief. Would the captain meet with the President of the United States and air his concerns? In a heartbeat.

At 5:30 the next morning, the captain presented the facts to Franklin Roosevelt at a brief pre-dawn meeting. During the next thirty days, whenever the president met with his military advisers, he inserted into his discussions the question of gunnery command in the event of an aerial attack. The constant pressure initiated a spiral of activity that led to the discovery of the naval captain's proposal and a permanent change in naval tactical policies, which undoubtedly saved countless American lives from Kamikaze attacks during World War II.

Franklin Delano Roosevelt practiced strategic humility by sending out representatives to perform duties that, he admitted to himself, he could no longer perform. In this, as in countless other instances during his lengthy presidency, Franklin Delano Roosevelt not only received, but earned, the respect of the public as well as those who worked with him. His actions show the rest of us that humility represents not an admission of defeat but, instead, recognition that success stems as much from knowing what you don't know as from what you do.

♣ Allows for Continuous Learning

Frederick Douglass knew this truth even as a child. Beginning life in the most humble conditions imaginable, Douglass went on to become one of the most brilliant orators in American history and an author of a celebrated autobiography written before age thirty. Born into slavery in 1818, Douglass, like many other slave children, owned just one long shirt and got most of his daily nourishment from little more than cornmeal mush. Nothing would have been more undreamable than that such a child would ever learn to read, much less become a scholar and writer whose work would help eradicate slavery.

Frederick Douglass himself did not know precisely when his story began. All he really knew about his birth was that he was born in Maryland to Harriet Baily on the Homes Hill Farm, property of Aaron Anthony. During his childhood, Douglass witnessed many of the horrors of slavery. One night, awakened by screams, he peered through a crack in the kitchen wall at Holmes Hill Farm to see his beautiful Aunt Hester, stripped to the waist, being flogged by her raging master. The more Hester wept, the harder Anthony hit her. Later, Douglass would witness an even more inhuman act. Upon Aaron Anthony's death, his estate, including Douglass and the other slaves, went to his children. Some of these heirs, deeming Douglass' grandmother too old to perform useful work, sent her into the Maryland woods to die.

The rest of the Douglass family was scattered among the Anthonys, with Frederick, who was about seven at the time, going to Aaron Anthony's daughter, Sophia Auld. Douglass described his new mistress as "a kind and tender-hearted woman," so much so, in fact, that, encouraged by Douglass' keen intelligence, she began to teach him to read. When Sophia proudly told her husband of the child's astonishing progress, Hugh Auld forbade his wife to continue. A slave who could read and write would, Auld insisted, grow discontent with his position and become unfit to work as a slave. That's why teaching a slave to read and write was against the law.

Frederick Douglass overheard his new master's tirade and grasped the fact that if Auld so vehemently opposed a slave's learning to read, literacy must be a very valuable skill indeed. Sophia Auld, committed to playing the good wife, brought Douglass' education to an abrupt halt. With what Douglass called "tiger-like fierceness," she did an about-face with the young boy, becoming "even more violent in her opposition than her husband himself. She was not satisfied with simply doing as well as he had commanded; she seemed anxious to do better." Whenever she found Douglass with a newspaper, she snatched it away, but she could not, it turned out, douse the flame she had lit.

Whenever Douglass left the Auld estate on errands, he carried with him a book and some bread. Poor, hungry neighborhood white children eagerly traded their own meager knowledge of reading in exchange for the bread. The more he read, the more Douglass yearned for the freedom he could attain by escaping to the North. Since he might escape by forging a pass that would permit him to travel unattended, he resolved to add writing to his education. Once again, he cleverly sought the aid of others. Occasionally visiting the shipyard on his errands, he watched as the ship carpenters inscribed letters on each piece of timber indicating where it would fit into the ship's structure. For instance, "S" meant starboard; "L.A." meant larboard aft. Douglass practiced copying these letters. Then, whenever he encountered a boy who knew how to write, he would issue a dare: "I would tell him I could write as well as he." Douglass would write those letters he knew (at first, only S, L, A and F). While the other boy would always win the dare by writing more letters, Frederick Douglass won much more: he was learning how to write, a few letters at a time.

Douglass had endured terrible beatings working in the fields, but a beating he received once he became a shipyard apprentice set in motion a series of events that strengthened his resolve to escape. Hired out by his master to work as a caulker's apprentice, Douglass often suffered harassment at the hands of jealous white workers, who hated the idea of competing with slaves or free black men for jobs. One day, a group of white apprentices attacked Douglass, beat him severely, and nearly took out one of his eyes. An outraged Hugh

Auld tried to press charges, but since the courts would not accept the word of blacks against whites, none of the black workers who witnessed the beating could legally testify, and the crime went unpunished.

After a lengthy recovery from his wounds, Douglass returned to the shipyard, each week handing over his pay to his master. When he returned from work late one day, Auld flew into such a rage that Douglass finally resolved to escape. In three weeks, on September 3, 1838, he would board a train for the North.

Though most escape attempts ended tragically, Douglass managed to travel safely to freedom in the North. Once there, he involved himself in the abolitionist movement, and soon began speaking passionately for the cause. His orations captivated his listeners, so much so, in fact, that the leaders of the abolitionist movement suggested he try to sound less learned, lest his audiences begin doubting that he could have really come from the humble and terrible background he described.

In response, Douglass wrote the *Narrative of the Life of Frederick Douglass, an American Slave,* in which he named names and provided locations and dates to prove the truthfulness of his story. This book, published in 1845, became a best-seller in the North and won the author fame in England, where he subsequently went to speak. Even more achievements lay ahead, as he founded the anti-slavery newspaper *North Star* and became a trusted adviser to Abraham Lincoln during the Civil War.

Strategic humility initiated Douglass' career as spokesman, editor, writer, political activist and presidential adviser. From the beginning, he knew where he wanted to go and, each step of the way, he admitted that he needed the help of others to get there. In a world where things almost always went wrong for African Americans, Frederick Douglass made things go right, not just for himself, but for the millions of people whose lives his words touched and continue to touch.

♣ Provides a Role Model

Unlike Frederick Douglass, Jane Addams began her life in the security of a well-positioned family. Born in Cedarville, Illinois in 1860, Jane did, however, share something in common with Douglass. Her father, John Addams, a successful businessman and politician, was a close friend of President Abraham Lincoln. John Addams raised Jane and his eight other children by himself after his wife's death. Although Jane Addams was a delicate child, she nonetheless went on to graduate at the top of her college class and enter a medical college with aspirations of becoming a physician. When problems with back pain forced her to drop out after her first year, she reevaluated her prospects and set her sights on helping people, just as she would have had she become a doctor. What could she possibly do? Frustrated and undecided, she departed for Europe with a friend, Ellen Starr, to see the world and consider her choices.

In England she and Starr visited a settlement house called Toynbee Hall in London's East End. Founded by Samuel Barnett in 1884, Toynbee Hall was the first community center established to combat the problems of urban poverty. The visit so inspired Addams and Starr that, upon their return to America, they leased a building in the heart of Chicago's worst immigrant slum, with the goal of using it as a home base for helping the city's poor.

The two young women called their organization Hull House, and once they moved in they immediately launched their campaign to improve conditions in the neighborhood. Addams and Starr spoke frequently about the neighborhood's problems, raised funds, and recruited young women from wealthy families to help in their endeavors. They established a day care program, took care of the sick, and provided a sympathetic ear and helping hands to anyone in need.

By its second year, Hull House served 2,000 people every week—almost around the clock. Young children attended kindergarten classes during the day, older children participated in activities during the after-noon, and adults enrolled in a pilot night school that offered instruction in English, since many of the peo-ple they served were immigrants. Addams and Starr had other ideas for Hull House, but knowing that they did not carry the political weight to instigate all of the changes for which they hoped, they enlisted the support of Chicago's intellectual elite, including the doctor Alice Hamilton and the great American philosopher John Dewey. With their help, Hull House established an art gallery, a public kitchen to provide hot lunches, an athletic facility for the neighborhood residents, a cir-culating library, and an employment service on the premises. Hull House encouraged its diverse neighbor-hood community to work together to improve their living conditions, while Addams petitioned the city to pave streets and build improved parks and playgrounds.

Addams' growing reputation for civic initiative soon brought her other opportunities. In 1905 she accepted an appointment to Chicago's Board of Education, and in 1909 she became the first woman president of the National Conference of Charities and Corrections. The next year Yale University offered her the first honorary degree it had ever awarded a woman. Indi-viduals involved in Hull House initiated studies of midwifery, narcotics use, and sanitary conditions. An enthusiastic advocate of women's rights, Addams also supported the suffrage movement and enhanced oppor-tunities for women in the workplace. She spoke for peace as World War I threatened to break out, giving a series of lectures at the University of Wisconsin, which she later published as a book, *Newer Ideals of Peace*.

Just as Toynbee Hall had provided an inspiration for her, Addams and her work served as a role model for the development of community centers across the United States. For these efforts, and for her international work in the name of peace, Addams won a Nobel Peace Prize on December 10, 1931.

Jane Addams died in May 1935, but her legacy lives on. She invented the concept of community activism. She accepted her physical limitations, set her goals high, and enlisted the help she needed to reach those goals. By practicing strategic humility, she made things go right.

♣ STRATEGIC HUMILITY AND THE NEW MURPHY'S LAW

Humility, far from signifying weakness or low self-esteem, signals extraordinary self-confidence. Recognizing and acknowledging our limitations, and admitting what we don't know or what we can't do allows us to replace pessimism with optimism. Things can only go right if we close the gap between what we know and what we don't know, and that usually means enlisting the help of others who know what we don't know or who can do what we can't do. The people we've met in this chapter exemplify the values of strategic humility, and their stories convey lessons we can all apply to our own lives.

♣ **Lesson 1: Define What You Don't Know or Can't Do.** Ben Cohen and Jerry Greenfield reached reached a point where they knew they lacked the knowledge and skill to continue growing their company, so they sought help without compromising their ideals. Have you ever pretended you knew how to do something then embarrassed yourself when you couldn't perform? Do you regularly consider what you need to know but don't know? Whenever you discover a gap, do you seek the help of others? Have you ever felt uncomfortable asking for help? Devote some time each day to defining what you need to learn in order to accomplish your goals and to listing possible sources of knowledge that could help you close the gap.

♣ **Lesson 2: Make the Most of What You Do Know**. As Chuck Jones would undoubtedly admit, he couldn't draw like da Vinci, but he could fashion cartoon characters who leapt from the screen into viewers' hearts. When you examine your knowledge and skills, can you see that you often possess more than you realized? Does someone else's superior knowledge or skill ever dishearten you? Do you try to uncover hidden knowledge or skills you've ignored in the past? Paradoxically, most of us both know less than we think and more than we realize. Try to consider both sides of that coin as you continue to move toward your goals.

♣ **Lesson 3: Respect Others and They Will Respect You**. FDR didn't lose respect when he relied on his "personal listeners," he gained it. Have you ever accepted as gospel the opinions of a superior just because of that person's rank? Conversely, do you ever dismiss the opinions of subordinates because of their lower position on the ladder? Does reliance on the opinions of those above or below you lower or raise your self-esteem? Respect engenders respect. People you ask for help will usually admire you for admitting and trying to overcome any lack of knowledge or skill.

♣ **Lesson 4: Look at Life as a Never-Ending Learning Experience**. Frederick Douglass learned to write one letter at a time, and he won converts to his cause one person at a time. At any point in your continuing education have you ever sat back and said, "That's all I really need to know"? Do you view every day as an opportunity to learn something new? Has it ever surprised you to find out that someone knows more about a subject than you do, even if you are a leading expert on that subject? Think of yourself as a student who every day goes to school eager to gain new knowledge and skills.

♣ **Lesson 5: Never Forget That Others Look to You for Help.** While Jane Addams used Toynbee Hall as a role model, she built Hull House into an even more influential model for community service. Do you remain open to teach, coach and mentor others who may need your help? Can you view yourself through the eyes of others and see yourself as they see you? Do your actions consistently provide a positive role model? A good teacher never abandons the role of student, and every good student accepts the role of teacher to those who need help. Act every day as a student-teacher.

As you ask yourself these questions, consider whether you need to change your goals, or look for ways to gain more knowledge and skills that will help achieve them. In either case, practice strategic humility and close the gap between what you know and don't know by seeking out those who can fill it.

Rule 6

Put Your Time Where It Really Counts

"Time is the most valuable thing that a man can spend."

Diogenes

♣ "DON'T WORRY, BE HAPPY"

Who doesn't know the title of Bobby McFerrin's song, the one that made his reputation in popular music? What many people don't know, however, is that "Don't Worry, Be Happy" does not even begin to represent the achievements and interests of this incredibly talented musician.

Bobby McFerrin knew all his life that he wanted a career in music. Born in New York in 1950, he began studying music at the age of six, and by the time he entered high school, he could play several instruments. McFerrin continued his musical studies throughout his formal education, first at California State University in Sacramento then at Cerritos College. After completing his college career, he plunged into a career as a vocalist.

Throughout his musical studies, as he learned to play a wide variety of musical instruments, Bobby McFerrin also developed an uncanny ability to imitate those instruments vocally. Friends and acquaintances were amazed at the seeming ease with which he could produce sounds that mimicked those of horns, drums, and even string instruments. McFerrin practiced and fine-tuned his vocal skills until even a trained musician could not tell the difference between a tune he produced with his voice and the same melody played on an instrument. A master vocalist unlike any the world of music had heard before, he quickly won recognition and success in a very tough business.

McFerrin spent a brief period of time as a member of a band called Astral Projections in New Orleans. Before long, however, he moved back to California, where he met Bill Cosby, who proved instrumental in bringing McFerrin to the jazz and popular musical forefront. Cosby, impressed by the young vocalist's originality and talent, arranged for McFerrin to perform at the Hollywood Bowl as part of the 1980 Playboy Jazz Festival. His appearance at that high-profile event led to further engagements, then to a recording deal with the Elektra/Musician label. By 1982, Bobby McFerrin had released his debut album followed by a widely acclaimed 1983 tour of unaccompanied vocal concerts.

Throughout the 1980s, McFerrin's popularity grew, peaking in 1988 with the release of "Don't Worry, Be Happy." On this upbeat track, McFerrin sang the lead and backup vocals, and used his voice to simulate traditional instruments.

Given his enormous popularity, Bobby McFerrin was perfectly on track with his life and career. Or was he?

The greater his success, the more he began to question whether it represented a true life priority and the best use of his time. McFerrin increasingly found popular music less fulfilling than his fans could possibly imagine. Given his classical training and his passion for orchestration, he felt increasingly drawn back to the classics.

McFerrin thus decided to stop doing what had made him famous and to reallocate his time to become an orchestra conductor. Although he knew that the road to acceptance within the world of classical music would take tremendous time and energy—not to mention overcoming the skepticism over his reputation as a popular musician—he threw himself completely into his new calling.

McFerrin studied diligently for his new career, working with renowned conductor Gustav Meier. Yes, he did encounter some resistance along the way, especially from people who did not believe that a "pop star" could possibly comprehend the finer points of classical music. Also, with his dreadlocks and quirky style of dress, McFerrin did not fit the standard public image of a classical conductor. Still, it did not take long for the new conductor to convince the classical music world that he could do the job—and do it marvelously.

He made his conducting debut in 1990 with the San Francisco Symphony and, within four years, he was widely accepted as a competent, skilled conductor—a reputation that won him appointment as Creative Chair of the St. Paul Chamber Orchestra (SPCO).

McFerrin's reputation continues to rise in the world of classical music. He has released several recordings as a conductor, has toured with the SPCO, and has appeared with the New York Philharmonic, the Chicago Symphony, the Cleveland Orchestra, and the London Philharmonic, among others. Even as he continues to tour, McFerrin has accepted a commission from the

San Francisco Opera to compose his first original opera score. McFerrin's reputation as a classical artist has become so established, in fact, that National Public Radio nominated him in 1997 for its Player of the Year Award—an award given to a conductor or other prominent figure who has served as an outstanding advocate for classical music.

Time. We all spend it, but do we always spend it wisely? Knowingly or not, Bobby McFerrin's time-life priorities followed a well-known law in the business world established by economist Wilfredo Pareto. Pareto's law states that, on average, only 20 percent of the tasks we perform each day are really necessary and fruitful. The remainder of our time, 80 percent, we largely fritter away on trivialities or unnecessary tasks. McFerrin inverted Pareto's Law: he spent most of his time on the things that really counted in his life. If spending 20 percent of your time can get you through your daily grind, why not spend 100 percent of your time going after what you really want? While we may not all achieve stardom, we can all certainly learn to use our time more wisely and efficiently, by following the example of Bobby McFerrin.

The following four strategies can help us do just that:

**FOUR STRATEGIES FOR INVESTING
YOUR TIME WISELY**

1 Look Before You Leap

2 Make the Most of Every Minute

3 Follow Your Heart

4 Practice, Practice, Practice

Do you ever find yourself wasting time because you didn't plan out a project or activity thoroughly enough?

When faced with only a short period of time to accomplish a task, do you focus your energies and streamline your activities in order to meet your deadline?

Have you ever found yourself devoting too much time to a task that you realized meant little to you? If so, have you managed to shift more resources to what really matters?

When a job requires a lot of time, perseverance and practice, do you follow it through with steadfast determination?

The people you will encounter in this chapter have met the challenge of allotting their time wisely and well, overcoming the ineffectual practices described by Pareto's Law. By following their examples, you, too, can learn to put your time where it counts.

♣ LOOK BEFORE YOU LEAP

Your initial investment of time in any project—that brief period during which you contemplate an activity before rushing headlong into it—can be the wisest one you make. Doing so sometimes requires a good deal of discipline, a self-control often hard to maintain before the battle commences. Haste can make waste—a truth we all know but often forget. In your eagerness to succeed at a task, you can easily waste that valuable pre-battle contemplation. Michael Silva did not. His story shows the value of being disciplined and, when appropriate, taking the time to plan how best to use your time in the future.

At the age of twenty-nine, Michael Silva became one of the youngest CEOs of a major corporation when he took the helm of Bennett Enterprises, a troubled $100-million conglomerate in Salt Lake City. Three years later he had turned the company around, converting years of losses into strong earnings, a feat he accomplished by "looking before he leapt" and pausing to reflect on how he could best leverage his time.

"Everyone expected me to be an out-of-control kid," Silva recalls. "Here was a 100-year-old company, basically an old-fashioned paint and glass manufacturer, that had been run by the Bennett family for longer than anyone could remember. And here I was, not yet thirty, and with a reputation for shooting first and asking questions later."

Silva grew up in Hawaii. An incredibly bright, precocious child, he wasted no time in getting through elementary and high school—at only fourteen, he entered the freshman class of Loyola University. Later, he studied business at Brigham Young University in Salt Lake City, then returned to Hawaii, where he learned finance from a Japanese banker. Eventually, he took a job developing banking strategies and crisis management techniques at Arthur Young, one of the largest management consulting companies in the country. His sharp mind and charismatic manner quickly moved him from consulting for banks with financially troubled corporate borrowers to working directly with the struggling companies in a "hands-on" role. In this capacity, he helped corporations develop innovative strategies to get back on their feet and satisfy their creditors. One of those companies was Bennett Paint and Glass.

When the banks told Bennett's board of directors to hire a new CEO to help turn things around, consultant Silva watched a parade of candidates apply for the job. "They were all older, very expensive and pessimistic," he says. "I had been itching to apply what I'd learned about management in a real pressure cooker, so I proposed doing it for half the money in half the amount of time, provided I had complete autonomy."

PUT YOUR TIME WHERE IT REALLY COUNTS

Shortly after Senator Wallace J. Bennett, the head of the family who had run the business for decades, hired the brash young consultant, the local business press jumped on the story. Surely this "Boy Wonder," as one reporter dubbed Silva, would begin shaking things up immediately. The business community held its breath, expecting Silva to use "slash and burn" techniques in his restructuring of Bennett Enterprises. The community's reaction was hardly surprising, given the circumstances: they knew that Silva was under pressure to turn the company around quickly.

Michael Silva, however, resisted the temptation to fulfill the skeptics' expectations and made only one immediate decision: to take a six-week vacation in Hawaii. Believing in his ability to come up with a creative strategy for the turnaround, and relying on the soothing waves of the Pacific Ocean and what his Japanese mentor had taught him about the value of meditation, he sat on a beach for six weeks, thinking about the situation.

During those weeks the Salt Lake media forgot the story, and the business community went on with business as usual. They were amazed when Silva returned, called a press conference, and announced the first step in Bennett's revitalization. The company would diversify, he said, and, as its first step, it would buy a bank.

In Silva's own words, "I adopted a non-traditional approach. The traditional turnaround would have involved changing strategy, slashing expenses, entrenching and directing energy inside the company." Instead, although he did alter the company's focus and cut its expenses, he expanded rather than contracted the business, spent his time outside rather than inside the company, and changed something few CEOs would have addressed—the corporation's basic mission and culture.

The Bennett culture had been mired in the past, positioning itself as a conventional manufacturer. Now it became innovative, moving into new areas, from architectural design to healthcare and computer services. Silva's plan swung into motion in January 1982, and by the end of that year Bennett had earned $1.1 million, compared to a $3 million loss the year before.

Michael Silva's story proves the value of pausing to reflect before you make a major decision or enter a new battle in life. We all engage in daily battles, be they starting a major new project, tackling a new job or entering into a new phase of our life. When we do, we often feel tempted to jump into the fray immediately because we want to get the job done, win the battle, and reap the rewards of victory. That's the time to pause, step back as Silva did, and meditate on the work ahead. In this case, by looking before he leapt, Michael Silva made things go right.

♣ MAKE THE MOST OF EVERY MINUTE

The name Thomas Edison instantly brings to mind his invention of the incandescent light bulb, the phonograph or the first moving picture camera. In total, however, Thomas Edison recorded approximately 1,300 patents, an amazing number for any one person. How did Edison manage to accomplish so much in one short lifetime? More than anything else, he was a genius at managing his time.

Thomas Alva Edison wasted no time discovering where his interests lay: he loved science and the process of experimenting to gain new knowledge. Of course, early on, his experiments did not always produce results. At the age of six, for example, the young Edison grew fascinated with the power of fire and, one day, decided to test that power by setting fire to his father's barn "just to see what it would do." What it did, of course, was burn to the ground, almost taking the young boy with it. This foray into the world of experimentation earned him no acclaim; instead, he received a public spanking in the village square from his irate father.

Undaunted by this embarrassing failure, Edison continued his childhood experiments: sitting on (and unintentionally crushing) a clutch of goose eggs to see if they would hatch, mixing chemicals in his basement, and feeding huge quantities of carbonated Seidlitz powders to a friend to see if the gas they created in the boy's stomach would make him fly.

Most everyone in Edison's small hometown considered the boy a little crazy. Even his father felt there was something not quite right with his son. Edison's mother, on the other hand, believed in him and encouraged him to continue his experimenting. At the same time, she realized that his scientific bent should receive skilled guidance. Therefore, for his ninth birthday, she gave her son a copy of Parker's *School of Natural Philosophy*, a book that could supply a logical basis for his experiments.

During the next few years, Edison sped through Parker's text and many others as he plunged toward his goal in life: making things happen that no one had made happen before. Soon he discovered the basic reality that he would need money in order to fund his endeavors. So when the opportunity arose for him to earn a steady income, Edison jumped at it. In 1859, the twelve-year-old would-be inventor took a job with the new railroad between Port Huron and Detroit, signing on as a newsboy aboard the train. For the next eleven years, he worked diligently at this "regular" job, devoting only his spare time to his experiments.

When Edison completed his rounds as newsboy, he would sneak off to a chemical lab he had set up in a little-used baggage car. When some of the chemicals in his mobile lab spilled, however, and set fire to the car, he immediately found himself out of work. Still needing to support himself and his experiments, he decided to move into the telegraph business, which had fascinated him for some time. He encountered one problem, however: not knowing Morse code, he could not send or receive messages on the telegraph.

Edison did not let this obstacle stop him. Rather, he spent eighteen hours a day learning Morse code and practicing how to send and receive telegraph messages. Within a couple of weeks, he set up his own business sending messages locally, in Port Huron, which earned him only a modest income, but did afford him ample time to experiment. In fact, he focused much of this time on getting to know the workings of the telegraph machine intimately.

Eventually, the meagerness of his income forced Edison to abandon his local telegraph business. For a time, he wandered from job to job, barely making enough to sustain himself. Finally, though, he found himself in the Western Union office in Boston, once again, sending telegraph messages. And once again, he used every spare moment to perform his own experiments.

Edison began tackling a project that all the experts in telegraphy believed impossible: developing a telegraph wire that could send and receive messages at the same time. During the lulls in his business day, Edison worked on this impossible invention and, in May 1868, he made it happen. Newspaper reports of the time declared him a miracle worker.

A few months later, frustrated at having to divide his time between what he needed to do to support himself and what he dreamed of doing instead, Edison finally took a daring step. He would, he resolved, become a full-time experimenter. He quit his steady job, realizing that he might endure hunger and deprivation for a time, but convinced that he could succeed in the long run. Edison suffered several disappointments when he couldn't sell his inventions or when deals fell through at the last moment. However, Thomas Edison never despaired. He knew he would eventually find the investors he needed. "You wait, they will come to me yet," he vowed.

Before long, Edison's avowal came true in the form of General Marshal Lefferts, a businessman for whom the inventor had briefly worked. Lefferts, foreseeing the financial possibilities in the young inventor's work, summoned Edison to his office one day to ask, "How much will you take for all those contraptions?" Edison thought about requesting $5,000, but feared his patron would think that amount exorbitant. After all, he had not sold anything since his two-way wire. So, Edison countered with the cautious reply, "Make me an offer, General." When Lefferts proposed $4,000, the inventor took it without a second thought. Imagine his surprise, then, when he received a check for $40,000; he had misheard the general's offer!

Edison knew exactly what he would do with this windfall; in 1871, he opened a workshop in Newark, New Jersey, where he and eighteen hand-picked workmen worked full-time on his inventions. With others to carry out the mechanics of the plans he devised, Edison expected to multiply his productivity.

Over the next three years, Edison's workshop produced a number of devices to improve the telegraphy industry, as well as stock tickers for Wall Street firms and other electrical equipment for Western Union. In 1874, after patenting scores of relatively minor inventions, Edison moved to a bigger workshop—his now-famous "invention factory" in Menlo Park, New Jersey—taking with him his staff of workmen and also hiring several university-trained scientists. Edison had, in effect, set up the very first working laboratory designed to streamline the entire invention process.

An improved telephone transmitter was the first major invention to come out of the Menlo Park lab, followed by a crude phonograph. Then came the electric light— an invention that tried Edison's perseverance and patience more than any other. Several inventors had been experimenting with creating a light powered by electricity. More than one had succeeded in creating a flash of light, but none had hit upon the appropriate material for a filament that would not burn out quickly. Edison, knowing that he needed a material that could withstand a tremendous amount of heat for an extended period of time, painstakingly tested hundreds of different materials to find just the right one.

His wise time-management proved central to Edison's genius. He spent his time where it really counted and avoided spending it where it didn't count. As a part of the filament project, for example, Edison needed to know the cubical content of an irregular glass bulb. Too busy to focus on it himself, however, he asked one of his college-educated engineers to figure it out. A week later, when Edison asked the learned man for the data, he received a formidable array of charts and figures but no result.

"How much longer will it take you to solve the problem?" asked Edison. When the engineer requested another week to complete his calculations, Edison replied, "Let me show you how to do it in a minute." He filled the glass bulb with water and stated, "*That's* your answer."

In this instance, as throughout his life, Edison demonstrated that he knew the value of time well spent, and the irretrievable waste of time squandered. Whatever tasks we tackle in our work or our lives, we should adopt this simple maxim: make the most of every minute.

♣ FOLLOW YOUR HEART

Oftentimes, once we've chosen a particular path in life, we hesitate to change direction; even if we've grown disillusioned with that path, we fear that we'll look back and regret all the time we wasted doing something we didn't really love. But, how much more might we regret *not* having taken the time to change direction? Edward Albee faced just such a dilemma.

Born in 1928 in Virginia, Albee was immediately put up for adoption. When he was only two weeks old, he was adopted by Reed and Frances Albee. As a member of the Albee clan, a well-known New York City-based theatrical family, he naturally began hanging around the theater at an early age. He loved the experience and to this day fondly remembers the performers and other "theater people" who filled his home.

While he thrived among the theater folk, he struggled in school. An indifferent student, he was expelled from more than one private school. Finally, as a student at the Choate School in Wallingford, Connecticut, he began to pursue his love of literature and the theater. His teachers saw potential in him and encouraged him to pursue his literary interests by enrolling in Trinity College in Hartford, Connecticut. However, after only three semesters, he found the experience stifling and dropped out of college.

Moving to Greenwich Village in New York City, he supported himself largely through a series of low-paying jobs, working variously as a book salesman, an office assistant, a messenger, and a record salesman. Ironically, he actually preferred working at these odd jobs and once said he especially liked working as a Western Union messenger, a job he held for three years, because "it could never possibly become a career."

Despite the humdrum routine of his work life, Edward Albee loved living in New York and sampling the vast cultural smorgasbord of concerts, art exhibitions, plays and more. He especially enjoyed the avant-garde plays of Eugene Ionesco and Samuel Beckett, who were developing an entirely new form of drama: Theater of the Absurd. Their plays, which explored the ridiculousness of society, captivated Albee, who had continued writing privately throughout his New York years, and propelled him to intensify his focus on writing.

The problem, obviously, was how to achieve this focus while attempting to hold down his messenger job. The answer came in the form of a unique birthday gift which he gave to himself when he turned thirty: he quit his job at Western Union, installed himself at his kitchen table with pen and paper in hand, and began writing a play.

Edward Albee's resolve paid off almost overnight. Once he began doing what he loved full-time, in less than three weeks he completed *The Zoo Story*, a one-act play about two strangers meeting in Central Park. Undaunted by several rejections from New York producers to stage the new play, the budding playwright widened his search and eventually drew the attention of German producers. Translated into German, *The Zoo Story* premiered in 1959 in West Berlin. Soon after, it made its American debut in Greenwich Village.

Albee would go on to create more than twenty-five plays over the next three decades, most of them dealing with the absurdity of the superficial concerns of modern life. His plays concentrate on the issue of time and the pathos of those who find themselves running out. "All my plays are about people missing the boat, closing down too young, coming to the end of their lives with regret at things not done." Too many people, he said, "sleep through" their lives, never fully taking the time to do what really matters most to them. This message struck a chord with audiences and literary critics alike. Three of Albee's plays have received the Pulitzer Prize for drama: *A Delicate Balance* in 1966, *Seascape* in 1974 and *Three Tall Women* in 1994. His most well-known play, *Who's Afraid of Virginia Woolf?*, became a classic film starring Elizabeth Taylor and Richard Burton.

Edward Albee could have kept wasting his time trudging down the path of routine, never testing his capacity to fulfill his life's priorities by refocusing the way he spent his time. Once he established his priorities, he was able to put his time where it really counted.

♣ PRACTICE, PRACTICE, PRACTICE

Anyone who has ever tried to hit a little white ball with an eight iron into a 4-and-a-half inch cup 120 yards away knows the meaning of frustration. Every day millions of people play golf around the world, but only a select few can land the ball close to the cup a hundred times in a row. Ben Hogan could, but not without practice.

Most golf lovers know the Ben Hogan legend, but not many know the story behind the legend. That story began at the outset of Hogan's professional career, when it appeared that he would never match the other stars on the tour.

Ben Hogan could always hit the ball a country mile— hitting for distance never posed a problem for him. Hitting it straight down the fairway did. His ball would soar off the tee, but it would always make a sharp hard left-hand turn—what golfers call a "hook." Hogan tried everything to correct his hook, hitting hundreds of balls day in and day out. That's when he began developing his legendary commitment to practice, practice, practice. Early in the morning, before most other golfers had even opened their eyes, Hogan could be found on the range trying to get a handle on that wicked hook. And long after other golfers had retired for the day, Hogan remained outside, precisely slugging away at those practice balls. Still, there they all went, bending sharply to the left.

Then, one evening in the fall of 1946, as Hogan lay in bed reflecting upon his recent practice sessions, reviewing his swing over and over in his mind, an answer to the problem quietly insinuated itself into his consciousness. He did not sleep at all that night; instead, he practiced his swing repeatedly in his mind, accustoming himself to the slight adjustment in form that he hoped would lay that persistent hook to rest.

At dawn, Hogan rose from his reveries, raced to the course, teed up a ball, envisioned the adjustments to his swing, and whacked it with all his might. As he followed its trajectory, Hogan saw it fly straight, not hooking at all but, in fact, slicing slightly to the right.

Hogan set about perfecting the improved trajectory, staying on the course for eight hours that day. "It was like learning to play golf all over again," Hogan recalled. But he learned well. "The harder I hit it," he rejoiced, "the better it worked." At the end of the week, Hogan traveled to Chicago for the Tam O'Shanter golf tournament, where he would try out his new discovery for the first time under all the stresses of tournament play. He won that tournament. All that practice had paid off.

Over the next several years, Hogan won so many tournaments that a furor erupted in pro-golf circles over the "secret" he had discovered that had enabled him to perfect his swing. What was "Hogan's secret"? He always claimed his secret was in the dirt, which translated to: practice twice as hard as anyone else.

In 1949, at the pinnacle of Hogan's success, tragedy struck when he and his wife were involved in a terrible auto crash. Hogan threw himself over his wife to save her, and came away with one leg so badly mangled that the doctors held out little hope that he would ever walk again—let alone play golf. In fact, they held out little hope that he would ever get out of his hospital bed. Of course, "never" was not a word that Hogan would ever accept.

He had worked so long and hard to achieve his goal, he was not going to let a crippled leg stop him now. Though it took some time, Hogan did indeed rise from his hospital bed and, not long after, he returned to the golf course and began to practice again. This time, Hogan really did have to learn to play the game all over again. The stance he had practiced for so many grueling hours could not accommodate the knee injury he'd suffered in the accident.

For months, Hogan could be seen trudging around the local golf course hour after hour, dragging his injured leg behind him. Throughout the rest of his life he would walk with a limp. Still, he practiced and practiced and practiced until he felt ready to rejoin the professional tour. When he did rejoin it, Hogan stunned the golf world by quickly regaining his top ranking. Although his doctors, his peers, and the public may have written him off for a time, Ben Hogan never lost faith in the power of practice. In fact, with a total of sixty-three victories, the overall success of Ben Hogan's career, both before and after the accident, remains virtually unparalleled today.

♣ TIME
AND THE NEW MURPHY'S LAW

We often ask ourselves at New Year's, at the end of another summer, or even at the end of a pleasant weekend, "Where has the time gone?" Indeed, we all know how easily time can get away from us, with hours, days, months, and even years seeming to pass in the blink of an eye. Nevertheless, we can choose to manage our time rather than let it manage us. To make things go right, we must be able to put our time where it counts. The lessons from this chapter help.

♣ **Lesson 1: Keep Your Eye on the Prize**. Bobby McFerrin set a new goal for himself then concentrated on achieving it. Have you ever let resistance, distractions, or setbacks prevent you from moving steadily toward your goal? Do you try to minimize distractions and interruptions? If you maintain your focus on your ultimate destination, as McFerrin did, you can see more clearly which activities really count, and which don't.

♣ **Lesson 2: Plan Your Work, Work Your Plan**. When everyone expected him to act brashly, Michael Silva took a vacation and thought long and hard about what to do when he returned home. Do you give yourself the time to lay careful plans before you begin a project or task, visualizing the steps you will take, or do you tend to jump into the project just to get things going? Have you ever wished you had designed a better plan before you sprang into action? If you feel anxious to get moving, discipline yourself to pause and look before you leap.

♣ **Lesson 3: It's Not the Time You Spend, It's How You Spend Your Time**. Thomas Edison valued both sides of time's coin: he concentrated his attention on what really mattered and shunned what didn't. Do you consistently set and reevaluate priorities, separating activities that count from those that don't? Have you ever let circumstances force a change in your priorities? If so, was the change productive or not? With a goal in mind and a solid plan in hand, you should keep asking yourself if you have your priorities straight.

♣ **Lesson 4: Do What You Love, Success Will Follow**. Edward Albee obeyed his heart when it told him to reclaim his first love—the theater. Have you ever turned your back on a dream because you let your head overrule your heart? Can you honestly say you've never felt regret over not having followed your dream, even if that dream somehow seemed impossible? Consult your heart, discover your passion, don't let logic always win out over your feelings: it's always more rewarding to pursue a love and lose than never to love at all.

♣ **Lesson 5: Keep Hitting the Ball Until You Hit It Straight**. Ben Hogan practiced harder than anyone else, never skipping a day of practice. Do you ever do something enough to get fairly good at it but not enough to get really good at it? Have you ever given something up because you found the necessary practice too frustrating or time-consuming? Practice may not make perfect, but it can make things go right.

In this fast-paced world of ours, we can so easily feel time-starved. There's just so much to do and so little time to do it all well. Time can become an enemy, but it can also become an ally if you invest it wisely and put it where it really counts.

Rule 7

Throw Anger Away

"Anger, then, is not merely a feeling or a bodily response, it is an orientation to the world."

Jonathan Lear

♣ A SONG IN HER HEART

Medical research has proven that anger can, quite literally, kill us. When our anger rises, our adrenaline flows, our blood pressure shoots up, and our rational thinking shuts down. Just as anger can precipitate a medical stroke, it can also paralyze our ability to face and overcome those events in our personal and work lives that made us angry in the first place. Whether caused by circumstances beyond our control or by our own actions, our anger can kill our chances of making things go right unless we learn how to "throw it away."

Despite a series of tragedies she could have easily let fuel her anger and resentment, Gloria Estefan has kept a song in her heart. Trouble started early for the Cuban-born superstar. In 1959, when she was only two years old, she and her family fled Havana after Fidel Castro unseated dictator Fulgencio Batista. Flying to Miami on a $21 flight with little more than the clothes on their backs, they settled in a Cuban ghetto behind the Orange Bowl. In 1961, her father, serving as a tank commander during the disastrous Bay of Pigs invasion, was captured and jailed in Havana. Eventually, in 1963, he was released; after returning to Miami, he joined the U.S. Army and went to Vietnam in 1967.

By this time, little Gloria Fajardo was spending hours sitting on her bed playing traditional Cuban tunes and Beatles singles on her guitar. Her father returned from the war the following year seriously impaired by the effects of Agent Orange. Gloria, then eleven, helped to nurse and feed and clean him until his hospitalization in 1976.

In 1975, while a student at the University of Miami, Gloria met her future husband, Emilio, at a wedding where his band, the Miami Latin Boys, was performing. After relenting to Emilio's coaxing that she sing a couple of songs, she ended up accepting his offer to join the group. Later, they formed a new band, the Miami Sound Machine, which combined Afro-Cuban dance rhythms with American pop. As Emilio recalls, "She was sad because of her father. The only moments I saw her happy was when she sang. Her eyes would come alive." While she eventually achieved fame and fortune with her singing, dangerous setbacks threatened her success every step of the way.

Gloria's father died in 1980, the same year that Gloria gave birth to her and Emilio's first child, Nayib, and the Miami Sound Machine landed its first record contract. Hit followed hit on the top of the charts for the only Latin artist to have enjoyed major crossover success. But the road ahead proved treacherous. After a semi-trailer rear-ended her tour bus on a snowy Pennsylvania highway in March 1990, Gloria regained consciousness to find herself temporarily paralyzed by a broken back. Emilio had also received serious injuries in the accident, and Nayib, then nine, suffered a broken collarbone. After an operation, Gloria underwent excruciating year-long physical rehabilitation—a pair of eight-inch titanium rods still brace her spine—only to encounter yet another ordeal.

Following Gloria's recovery, the Estefans tried for months to conceive a second child, without success. Tests showed that the collision had damaged one of her fallopian tubes. Fortunately, an operation corrected the problem, and, a month later, daughter Emily was conceived. With the birth of their second child in December 1994, the Estefans, it seemed, had dealt with the worst life could throw their way.

But the next year brought yet another disaster. On September 24, as the Estefans embarked on a pleasure cruise near Miami Beach, they watched in horror as law student Maynard Howard Clarke, twenty-nine, accidentally crashed his Wave Runner into their thirty-three-foot motorboat, suffering fatal lacerations when he hit the propellers. Emilio dove into the water and kept Clarke afloat as Gloria dialed 911, but Clarke died before he reached the hospital.

Despite so many difficulties encountered on her road to success, Gloria Estefan and her husband Emilio have prospered because they never let the sour notes obliterate the beautiful music in their lives. Although no one could have blamed either of them had they complained of the hardships they have suffered, the two chose never to let a setback ignite their anger.

To be sure, potential causes of anger disrupt our lives every day: a thoughtless insult by a boss, an injury or an illness, the contempt of a rival, or any other of the "slings and arrows of outrageous fortune" that beset us in this world. However, truly successful people resist the temptation to lose control through anger in such situations, and, like the Estefans, learn to channel it in a positive and creative way.

When confronting situations or people who try our patience, hurt our feelings or somehow threaten us, we can choose to let anger control and damage us, or we can choose to throw anger away, maintaining our own control over the course our lives will take.

In this chapter, we will explore four common sources of anger:

FOUR SOURCES OF ANGER

1 Born to Fail
2 Lightning Strikes
3 You Screw Up
4 Et Tu, Brutus?

While these four sources of anger by no means encompass all the ways in which we might feel tempted to lose our temper, they do represent situations most of us encounter at one time or another in our lives.

Have you ever felt that you were "born to fail," that life has dealt you an unfair hand by virtue of birth, race, color, creed, poverty or a mental or physical disadvantage?

How do you respond when "lightning strikes"—when an unexpected challenge gets in the way of your ambitions and desires?

When "you screw up," make an honest mistake, or do something foolish, do you punish yourself over the transgression?

Does the treachery or folly of others ever cause you to echo Caesar's words to his assassin, *"Et tu, Brutus?"*

As we examine these four sources of anger, we will observe real people choosing creativity over resentment, self-reliance over self-pity. Through their stories, you, too, can discover ways to throw anger away and thereby more easily make things go right whenever they go wrong.

♣ BORN TO FAIL

Life is not fair. How many times have we uttered those words to ourselves as we bemoaned our "bad luck"? Maybe our parents couldn't afford to send us to the best college, or perhaps a mental or physical disadvantage prevented us from doing what others do naturally. In such situations, we may think that we have every right to feel angry. Despite these feelings, however, we can choose a different path. Rather than indulge our frustration and ire, lashing out at others, or burying our feelings inside and letting them fester, we can move forward with a positive attitude. In short, we can allow our anger to take control of our lives—or we can choose to take control of our anger.

Most of us know that bursting into a fit of temper or pouting over a bad situation serves no productive purpose, but we also find it hard to react reasonably when we get angry. Frankly, sometimes raving about the unfairness of the world provides a certain amount of relief. Other times shame or embarrassment may tempt us to hold our feelings inside. The New Murphy's Law, however, dictates that self-indulgence does nothing to improve our lives. Rather, it suggests that we avoid feeling sorry for ourselves over our hardships, and that we strive to overcome whatever so-called "handicaps" life has dealt us. Sure, you can acknowledge that life can be unfair, but you need not allow that fact to paralyze you. Rather than sulking when it seems that fate has forsaken you, you can move past your anger to make something right out of even the greatest wrongs that befall you.

Many of Michigan businessman Don Barden's challenges in life fell into place before he was even born, giving him a built-in excuse to rail at the inequities that exist in the world. Barden was the ninth of thirteen children born to a poor African American family in rural Inkster, Michigan. With little outside income to support the family, everyone in the Barden household had to pull his or her own weight. All the children worked on the family's farm, raising pigs and chickens and growing vegetables in order to put food on the table.

Don Barden could easily have allowed himself to resent the hardship he endured as a child. Instead, though, he saw his humble beginning as an opportunity to learn an important lesson about life. "We were poor but determined," he reflects now. "My parents instilled in me a resolve to achieve and the work ethic to make it happen." Barden moved forward by getting a job as soon as he could. On one of his earliest jobs, toiling in the back room of an auto parts store, rebuilding engine parts, Barden learned yet another lesson. He remarks, "I noticed that the owner of the store was up at the front counter with a beautiful white shirt on, making all the money, and I was the guy in the back doing all the hard work."

While Barden may have felt a little resentment over this inequity, he did not let himself get caught up in negative feelings. Rather, he drew strength from this early working experience because it "gave me the motivation to try to be successful with my own business."

Although his positive outlook took hold quickly, the success he desired did not come easily. Yet a few more hurdles stood in his way. After scraping together enough money to get himself into college, he took a big step forward, but when the money ran out after only one year, he had to take a couple of steps back. He then held a series of odd jobs—as a mover, a laborer at a plumbing and heating company, a short order cook, and a shipbuilder. Throughout this period, he never let frustration deter him from his ultimate goal: owning a business of his own. Finally, Barden managed to set aside enough money to open Donnie's Record Shop. Only a year later, he founded a weekly newspaper, then, in 1968, a public relations and advertising firm. Don Barden, the poor kid from Inkster, Michigan, was on his way. Later, he diversified his business holdings even further, into the real estate market, and today he is making forays into the communications and entertainment industries.

The young man who envied the boss' clean, white shirt at the auto parts store, and who had to leave school when the money ran out, is now worth more than $100 million. He is one of the wealthiest African American businessmen in the country, with even greater prospects ahead. In 1996, Don Barden's business revenues reached an incredible $93.2 million, and he expected to clear $130 million in 1997. Even so, Don Barden does not rest on his laurels. "I'm on a mission," he asserts, "to prove that a poor, young African American from a very large family, from humble beginnings, can rise to the top in America in a free enterprise system." By refusing to indulge in resentment over his difficult beginnings and the tough row he has had to hoe in his life and by thrusting anger aside and investing his energies in a positive way, Don Barden has made things go right. His motto? Born to succeed!

♣ LIGHTNING STRIKES

Regardless of the gifts or disadvantages bestowed upon us at birth, lightning, in the form of an accident, an illness, a natural catastrophe or the deliberate malice of an enemy, can strike us at any time. When it does, we usually find our courage severely tested by a sudden change in our lives over which we have no control. The resulting feelings of powerlessness can easily turn to rage.

Lightning struck James Brady on March 30, 1981, when a would-be assassin's bullet pierced his brain. The videotape of James Brady lying face down and twitching in a pool of his own blood has been seared into our national memory, but it broke no one's heart more than his wife Sarah's. Did she feel angry? Sure, she did. But almost instantly she channeled her personal anger into a greater social cause.

We all know about the Brady Bill, the gun-control legislation named for James S. Brady, the former White House press secretary, which mandates a five-day waiting period before the purchase of a gun so that local law enforcement agencies can check the background of the potential buyer. But few of us know that the bill would not exist without the tireless efforts of Sarah Brady, who, motivated initially by disgust with the laxity of existing laws and fury over a life-shattering calamity, spearheaded the movement toward stricter gun-control laws.

Sarah Brady's experience with guns began early in her life. Her father, an FBI agent, kept a gun for work, and also hunted for recreation—however, he maintained a healthy respect for guns and the damage they can inflict. Brady recalls her father exercising extreme caution when it came to the safekeeping of his weapons—so much, in fact, that she does not remember ever actually seeing his guns.

Sarah Jane Kemp attended the College of William and Mary in Williamsburg, Virginia, and graduated in 1964. She went on to work for four years as a teacher before becoming involved with the Republican Party in 1968, when she signed on as an assistant to the campaign director at the National Republican Congressional Committee. Shortly thereafter, Sarah met her future husband, James, when he came to the National Republican Congressional Committee seeking funds for a congressional campaign he was managing in Illinois. Soon after their initial meeting, the two fell in love and eventually married in 1973.

The couple continued to work for the Republican Party—Sarah in the offices of Republican congressmen and for the Republican National Committee, and James in the campaigns of various GOP candidates. During the 1980 election, James served as the director of public affairs for Ronald Reagan's presidential campaign, a job that led Reagan to appoint him to the post of White House Press Secretary.

To the Bradys, whose first child had been born one year earlier, life seemed glorious. They enjoyed a top position among Washington's social and political elite, a strong family, and a prosperous lifestyle. How could anything possibly go wrong?

On March 30, 1981, just a few months after James assumed his position on the White House staff, something went very wrong. On that day, James Brady, along with several other White House staff members, accompanied President Reagan to the Washington Hilton Hotel, where the president spoke before a labor convention. As the group exited the hotel, gunshots rang out from only a few feet away. John W. Hinckley Jr., who would later be found mentally incompetent, had attempted to assassinate the president in a deranged plot to impress actress Jodi Foster, with whom he had been obsessed since seeing her in the movie *Taxi Driver*. Four people, including Reagan, were wounded in the assassination attempt, but James Brady suffered the worst injuries when a bullet pierced his forehead, above his left eye.

Sarah Brady first learned of her husband's injury on television news. Rushing to the hospital to comfort her husband when he emerged from surgery, she kept vigil at his side for hours. The bullet, it turned out, had destroyed 20 percent of James Brady's brain, leaving his left arm and leg permanently paralyzed. Luckily, James' mental faculties remained largely intact. He did, however, suffer some memory loss and a good deal of speech impairment, with which he continues to struggle.

In the days and weeks that followed, Sarah Brady stuck by her husband's side, helping him improve his condition and regain as much normalcy in his life as possible. She might have stayed home and never reentered the public arena if another near-tragedy had not struck her family.

While on a trip to Illinois to visit friends and family, Scott Brady, the couple's only son, clambered ahead of her into the cab of a friend's pickup truck and grabbed what appeared to be a toy gun lying on the front seat. As Sarah watched her son playfully point the gun at her, she immediately realized that he was not handling a toy, but a .22 caliber pistol—ironically, the same kind of inexpensive revolver that John Hinckley had used to shoot her husband. Sarah remained calm, gently taking the gun away from her son, but the incident shook her to the core of her being. As she related to Wayne King, who wrote a profile of the Bradys, she "stormed about it for days and weeks."

Sarah Brady transformed that personal fury into a public outcry when, upon returning to Washington, she learned that Congress was contemplating revising the Gun Control Act of 1968—not to strengthen it, but to nullify key provisions. She could not believe that any legislator would want to eliminate such common-sense clauses as the ban on mail-order gun sales and the requirement that gun dealers simply record the names of buyers. Irate, but determined to stop the nonsense, she phoned a gun-control advocacy group, Handgun Control, Inc., and asked what she could do to help.

Sarah Brady began by writing letters to members of Congress. She then lobbied in person on Capitol Hill. Soon she found herself delivering speeches across the country, tirelessly arguing for further restrictions on the availability of handguns. Her own tragic experiences with such weapons made her a highly compelling figure in the gun-control debate. As she explained to Barbara Gamarekian in an interview for the *New York Times*, "John Hinckley walked into a Dallas pawnshop and in minutes purchased a handgun. He committed a felony when he used a false address, but it went unnoticed because there was no requirement in Texas that his statements be verified."

Although Sarah Brady effectively conveyed her message, she faced a formidable opponent in the National Rifle Association, whose opposition helped defeat the Brady Bill in September of 1988. Did that anger Sarah? Surely. But it also strengthened her resolve. By 1990 her continuing efforts began to pay off. The Brady Bill and an accompanying ban on assault weapons were endorsed by the House of Representatives' Judiciary Committee, which meant that, by all rights, these proposals should come before the full House for a vote. The Bradys believed that they had mustered the votes to pass both bills. Disappointingly, however, neither piece of legislation was scheduled for a floor vote during that congressional session. The Speaker of the House asserted that the issue was too controversial to take up so late in the session, but he promised action early in the next Congress.

Once again overcoming her frustration and anger, Sarah Brady continued to lobby for the passage of these bills; finally, on November 10, 1993, the House passed an amended version of the Brady Bill by a vote of 238 to

189. Thanks in no small part to Sarah Brady, the Brady Law went into effect on February 28, 1994. During the first month of its implementation, a total of 23,610 people were prevented from purchasing guns, according to a survey by the Federal Bureau of Alcohol, Tobacco, and Firearms. Perhaps most significantly, one year after the law went into effect, statistics from the Federal Bureau of Investigation showed more than a 3½ percent drop in the number of handgun murders nationwide.

Lightning *will* strike. When it does, we can either let it destroy us, or we can seize control of the situation—as Sarah Brady did—to make even the most awful wrongs go right.

♣ YOU SCREW UP

It's only human to get mad at yourself when you make a mistake. After all, you can't blame your parents or the circumstances of your birth when you screw up, nor can you chalk it up to fate or bad luck. No, the responsibility for the situation lies squarely and heavily upon your own shoulders. You may, justifiably, feel disappointment in yourself and even indulge in self-accusations and self-hatred, but those feelings will not help you set things right; in fact, they may very well lead you to even greater folly. Instead, after acknowledging your error, you must move on and work to regain the ground you have lost.

Dan O'Brien faced precisely this situation. A young man seemingly on his way to great success in sports, O'Brien was raised in Klamath Falls, Oregon. Throughout his school years, he was a star athlete, making the All-State football team in high school and accomplishing even more in track-and-field. He was a natural. Given his talent at such a wide range of track events, his coach selected Dan to enter the national high school decathlon championship in his senior year. Considered by most athletes the most strenuous challenge in all of sports, the decathlon is a grueling combination of ten individual track-and-field events, including the 100-meter dash, 400-meter dash, long jump, shot-put, high jump, 110-meter hurdle, discus throw, pole vault, javelin throw, and 1,500-meter race. Although Dan lacked experience in pole-vaulting and all the throwing events, he won the championship title.

O'Brien's high school successes gained him a full scholarship to the University of Idaho in Moscow. The coach at the university, Mike Keller, believed he had discovered a born decathlete. Now the young star could receive training in the throwing events and the pole vault, which would surely cement his position as the best in the world. All he had to do was maintain a C-average to keep his place on the team.

Unfortunately, with the world at his feet, Dan O'Brien screwed up. Away from home for the first time in his life, he grew intoxicated with his new freedom and began to focus more on partying than on either his training or his studies. He drank too much and started using marijuana. When his grades came in below the required C-average, he lost his eligibility to compete in college sports. Then, in the fall of 1986, after three years of struggling to stay off academic probation, he lost his scholarship.

Desperate now and unwilling to face the shame of returning home, O'Brien held on to the electronic key card that provided access to his dormitory and the college cafeteria. He couldn't elude detection for very long, however, and that winter, the campus police removed him from the campus, throwing both him and his belongings into the street. Luckily, a friend let Dan stay at a nearby apartment during Christmas break. O'Brien later commented to Bob Wischnia, who wrote a profile of him for *Runner's World* magazine in May 1992, "I was so disgusted with my life that I couldn't go home to face my family. Everyone at school had gone home, but I stayed here all alone, rolling joints and drinking beer." Somehow, during this bleak period, Dan realized that he had made a terrible mistake; and, for a brief time, he feared that he could never get back on track. Disappointed in himself for the immaturity he had displayed and angry with himself for his own foolishness, he finally resolved to change his life for the better.

Early in 1988, he went to his former coach, Mike Keller, and asked for help. He knew that turning his life around would not be easy, and that he couldn't do it on his own. The coach told O'Brien that he would have to regain his life one step at a time, and he urged the young man to begin by enrolling at a local junior college; he even offered to help with tuition.

Taking his coach's advice, O'Brien enrolled for the spring 1988 school term at Spokane Community College, dedicating himself to success this time around: he regularly attended classes and worked out with the college's track team. In addition, O'Brien got a job at a local golf shop in order to pay back the $5,000 he owed the University of Idaho for his room and board during the period he had been sneaking into the dorm and cafeteria.

After O'Brien became eligible once again to participate in track meets due to his improved grades, he went on to win five events, including the decathlon, at the Northwest Junior College Championships. After only one semester at Spokane Community College, O'Brien gained readmittance to the University of Idaho in the fall of 1988. He wasn't allowed to compete with the track team until the spring term, but when he did compete, he won both the high hurdles and the long jump events at the Big Sky Conference Indoor Championships.

THROW ANGER AWAY

Dan O'Brien's newfound success in college-level sports restored his self-esteem and confidence. He dreamed, as many athletes do, of setting world records and winning Olympic gold. He told Wischnia that at that moment, "I could see that if I put the practice time in, I could be really good." O'Brien put in the time and, after some ups and downs in his track career, he finally realized his first dream at a 1992 decathlon meet in Talence, France.

The decathlon is scored by allotting a certain number of points to each event. The world record of 8,847 had been held for eight years by Daley Thompson of Great Britain. At the Talence meet, O'Brien excelled in every event, topping his own previous bests in the shot-put, the discus throw, and the javelin throw—events he had considered his weakest. When he crossed the finish line in the last event—the 1,500-meter run—he emerged with a score of 8,891 points, a new world record.

Four years later, at the Olympic Games in Atlanta, Georgia, Dan O'Brien finally made his second dream come true, when he won an Olympic gold medal in the decathlon in front of a cheering, proud audience of Americans. O'Brien described the dedication and determination it had taken to reach this pinnacle when, upon his victory, he said to Christine Brennan of the *Washington Post*, "This is what I thought about every single day for four years, winning the gold medal in Atlanta."

Dan O'Brien acknowledged his mistakes and then worked hard to move past them. Had he allowed himself to remain in that apartment in Moscow, Idaho, angry with himself and punishing himself for his mistakes, continuing to abuse alcohol and drugs, he would only have compounded his failure both as an athlete and as a man. However, Dan O'Brien determined to reverse the course of his life. Instead of wasting his seemingly boundless energy in self-destruction, he restrained it and then retrained it. In so doing, he fulfilled his own dreams and bolstered the pride of the entire nation.

♣ Et Tu, Brutus?

Confiding a secret to someone and having him or her turn around and quickly spread the word to others, overhearing a cutting remark made by a friend about you, having a great idea stolen and presented to the boss by a coworker—these sorts of betrayals can make anyone see red. Such relatively minor forms of treachery may do little to disrupt our lives, but they can cause a tremendous amount of pain. How can we work past our anger in order to move on with our lives? Consider the case of Nicole Contos.

In 1996, Contos, a kindergarten teacher from New York City, took the trip of a lifetime during her summer vacation, heading off to Greece for fun and relaxation. As it turned out, she found all that and more. In fact, when Nicole Contos returned to the United States, she believed she had found the love of her life.

During her vacation that August, Contos met a dashing British lawyer, Tasos Michael, on a Greek beach. Michael was a world traveler, a sophisticated and cosmopolitan man who swept the Manhattan schoolteacher off her feet.

Contos and Michael began dating and, before long, they were engaged to be married. The date was set for a little over a year after their first meeting, the church was booked and the invitations mailed. The couple experienced, inevitably, some last-minute jitters, but no real sign of trouble appeared. In fact, Contos said of her fiancé on their wedding day, "I spoke to him at noon. He said that his feet were like jelly, but he also said he'd bought tuxedo shoes."

Tasos Michael did wear those shoes, but not to dance at the reception. He was seen leaving Nicole Contos' apartment around noon on the day of the wedding, decked out in his tuxedo, but he never showed up at the Manhattan cathedral where he was to wed Nicole, and where Contos, along with dozens of friends and relatives, waited. Instead, Michael headed to the airport, using one of the tickets he had bought for his and Nicole's honeymoon trip and jetting off to Fiji—solo.

Tasos Michael left word with his best man that he was not planning to show up for his own wedding. About twenty minutes after the wedding was to have started, a frantic Nicole Contos heard the news. She then faced the intimidating task of making her very private betrayal public: she had to tell the guests waiting impatiently in the cathedral that there would be no wedding.

Contos might have left this chore to someone else in order to avoid embarrassment. She could have sequestered herself and indulged in her anger and grief in private. Nicole Contos, however, rejected the stereotypical responses of the "jilted bride"—instead, she changed into a short skirt and exhorted the guests to come to what would have been her wedding reception, but which Nicole turned into a lively party.

Word of Contos' positive reaction to an awkward situation spread, first around New York, and then around the country, on both local and national news shows. The story of Nicole Contos' enthusiastic dancing to the 1970s disco hit, "I Will Survive," hours after she was inexplicably betrayed by Tasos Michael provides a perfect image of someone conquering a sense of betrayal. Despite all the hurt and anger she must have felt over Michael's disappearance, she was bound and determined not to allow the treachery to ruin her life.

♣ ANGER
AND THE NEW MURPHY'S LAW

Whatever the source of your own anger—a circumstance of birth, an unexpected crisis, a stupid mistake, a betrayal, or any of the other setbacks in life that can ignite your ire—you can learn some valuable lessons from the people you've met in this chapter. To throw anger away and make things go right, you can do what they did:

♣ **Lesson 1: Make Anger a Temporary Emotion.** Gloria Estefan kept a song in her heart whenever tragedy struck. Have you ever let a misfortune so preoccupy your mind that it began to dominate your life and prevent you from moving forward? Do you attribute feelings of anger to some inherent flaw in yourself, believing that you can never overcome obstacles or disadvantages? Whenever you do, step back to see the big picture, the path of your life before and after the tornado struck, because doing so enables you to make anger only a temporary emotion.

♣ **Lesson 2: Keep Your Eye on Your Ultimate Goal.** If Don Barden had not stayed the course, envisioning his destination at every turn in the road, he would not have succeeded so spectacularly. Do your flaws or mistakes or the obstacles you face ever tempt you to abandon your dreams? Have you ever given up because the results you desire don't seem worth the effort anymore? If so, reaffirm your dream and rededicate yourself to getting the results you want. Life's circumstances may change, but they should not cause you to set your sights lower.

♣ **Lesson 3: Channel Your Feelings in a Positive Direction.** Rather than letting bitterness control her life, Sarah Brady channeled her feelings into an important cause. In a crisis do you tend to make matters worse by reacting negatively to negative events? Have you ever compounded a misfortune by adding the fuel of anger to the flames? When lightning strikes, bear in mind that two wrongs don't make a right, two negatives never add up to a positive.

♣ **Lesson 4: Learn from Your Mistakes.** Dan O'Brien's triumph came about because he vowed not to compound his mistakes by repeating them. When you screw up, do you ever deny what you did in an attempt to forget it and move on? Can you honestly say that you have never made the same mistake twice? Failure can teach us more than success because mistakes test our character, but denying our mistakes dooms us to repeating them. Define every mistake you make as an opportunity to learn and to grow.

♣ **Lesson 5: Turn the Other Cheek.** Rather than seeing her betrayal as the end of her life, Nicole Contos used it as a springboard to the rest of her life. Do you react to betrayal by resolving to get even or get revenge? Does a betrayal cause you to distrust everyone, assuming that you must constantly defend yourself against the selfishness or malice of others? Revenge and mistrust are the ugly stepchildren of anger. When someone slaps you in the face, you'll gain more by turning the other cheek than you ever will by multiplying the negative emotions surrounding a betrayal.

Observing these five lessons will not solve your problems, nor will they keep a new source of anger from ambushing you tomorrow. However, they will help you channel the energies that could go into anger into positive action, protecting the optimism embodied in the New Murphy's Law, and the belief that no matter what goes wrong in life, you can make it go right by throwing anger away.

Rule 8

Do The Right Thing

"The only obligation which I have the right to assume is to do at any time what I think is right."

Henry David Thoreau

♣ GOOD BEGETS GOOD

Some people call it karma, others simply say, "What goes around, comes around." Whatever the expression, the idea remains the same: those people who do good for others usually receive the same in return. The individuals in this chapter made things right in their own lives by doing what was right for others.

Kip Keino, a medal-winning runner from Kenya, has shelves full of trophies and awards, including two gold and two silver Olympic medals. Keino became a national hero on October 20, 1968, when he won his first Olympic laurels in the 1,500-meter race at the

Olympic Games in Mexico City. Although he was suffering from stomach pains (later diagnosed as a severe gallbladder infection), Keino ignored his doctors' advice to withdraw from competition. He had made a commitment to represent his country, and he would let nothing stand in his way. Ten days before, he had attempted to run the 10,000-meter race only to collapse in pain on the infield before he could cross the finish line. Officials had sent for the stretcher, but before it could arrive, Keino had staggered to his feet to finish the race even though he had been disqualified for leaving the track. Four days later he summoned the strength to race in and win a silver medal in the 5,000-meter race.

Expectations ran high at the start of the 1,500-meter race. What would this amazing Kenyan manage to pull off today? At the starting line of the race, Kip says that he became so focused on his performance that "without a video, I wouldn't know what happened at the finish." Kip was competing against his main rival, Jim Ryun, an American powerhouse on a three-year winning streak; even a perfectly healthy Keino would have faced a difficult challenge. However, the Kenyan pulled out fast from the very beginning, and he never lost his lead. Jim Ryun finished twenty meters behind his rival to capture the silver.

In his native country, Kip immediately became a national hero. Streets were named after him, commendations were showered on him, and his legend became secure when he won another gold medal and a silver four years later in the Munich games.

While these athletic achievements won him fame, they are by no means Kip Keino's only claim to greatness. In fact, if you asked him to cite the most rewarding accomplishment in his life, he would not even talk about running fast. Even while he was busily training and competing in grueling international competitions,

Keino, along with his wife, Phyllis, were making a much greater contribution to their world.

Thirty years ago, Kip and his wife, with seven children of their own, began taking orphans into their home in the town of Aldoret in northwestern Kenya. They began by taking in a few children brought to them by friends on the local police force. Before long, however, the Keinos found dozens of youngsters crammed into their small house. At that point, Kip Keino wrestled with a dilemma: either turn down the next child in need who came to his attention or relocate to a larger home. Keino's heart was too big to allow him to say no when a child needed him. So, he chose to find a new home. All he needed was the money to finance it.

Despite his prominent status, Keino was by no means a wealthy man. He earned about $20,000 total during his years of competition, and he had set that sum aside to provide his family's security blanket. Now, he took this nest egg and invested it all in a farm and large dormitory that could accommodate more homeless children. When asked what inspired him to dedicate himself to raising so many of Kenya's unwanted children, Keino responds, "My mother died when I was three. I don't want anyone else to grow up with that problem. I can't help everyone, but I do what is within my ability."

That ability even outstripped his ability as a runner. True, he could not help all the abandoned children in the world, but Kip has managed to prevent an incredible number from languishing in government institutions, largely because he and his wife run the farm and orphanage so efficiently. Everyone works. In addition to their schoolwork, the children help out by performing various chores according to their age and ability—milking cows, and harvesting the corn, potatoes, cabbage, and other produce grown on the family's fields.

When the work creates a surplus, the Keinos sell it in order to obtain necessary cash. Still, they always seem to teeter on the edge of solvency. Luckily, good deeds beget good deeds. Church groups and Christian relief organizations from around the world, hearing of the Keinos' undertaking, have provided intermittent assistance, sometimes financial and sometimes in other ways. Volunteers from far-flung countries have come to the Keino farm to offer their time and labor, and individuals who admire the Keinos often send small cash donations of $10 or $20.

Thus far, Kip and Phyllis Keino have harbored and nurtured hundreds of children within the walls of their farmhouse and dormitory. Today, seventy-three children and young adults, ages two to twenty-two, live on the farm. "I think I have been lucky," Kip says. "Now what is important is how I use what I have to help others."

We hear so much in the media today about all the terrible things that people do to each other that we tend to forget that people like the Keinos exist. However, many like them do the right thing every day, demanding no special recognition or reward for their actions. They know that, while seldom the easiest or most expedient choice, by doing right for others they can make things go more right in their own lives. Four basic motives can propel us to do likewise:

FOUR MOTIVES FOR DOING RIGHT

1 Cleanse Your Conscience

2 Build Trust

3 Set a Precedent

4 Get Results

Are you willing to put yourself on the line in order to help those with whom you work and live? Do you rank a clean conscience as more important than any sacrifice you must make in order to make people's lives better?

Do you place the welfare of others above convenience and expedience? Do you value trust as highly as tangible rewards?

Can you say that you try to set a precedent for good behavior? Do you understand that your every action, good or bad, provides an example for others?

When you throw yourself behind a cause, do you stick with it until you get results?

Though doing the right thing may be inconvenient and require sacrifice, that sacrifice pales against the consequences of doing the wrong thing. Doing the wrong thing never makes things go right, as the following stories prove.

♣ CLEANSE YOUR CONSCIENCE

When Oscar Robertson offered his kidney to his ailing daughter, Tia, he did what he believes any father would do. What parent wouldn't do the right thing for a daughter, regardless of the personal sacrifice involved? But Robertson is not just any father—he is one of the greatest basketball players who ever played the game. Yet, when it came to his daughter's life, he did not act as many celebrities would, turning the situation into a publicity event—another photo opportunity to revive the public image. Robertson did exactly the opposite— he did the right thing as an act of love, pure and simple.

Long before Michael Jordan came on the scene, no one handled the ball with as much understated aplomb and efficiency as the "Big O"—Oscar Robertson. In his fourteen-year professional career, he made 9,887 assists under the kind of pressure that players today don't encounter. As a young NBA player during the early '60s,

Robertson endured racial taunts, and worse, from fans in cities like Tulsa and Raleigh. Nor had it been easy when he took the court as the first nationally recognized black athlete at the University of Cincinnati. Recently, though, in honor of his achievements there, the university erected a nine-foot-high statue of Robertson. True to his reputation for understatement and discretion, Robertson reacted with more embarrassment than pride.

He behaved just as discreetly in April 1997, when he and his daughter registered at Cincinnati's University Hospital under assumed names for the kidney transplant. The story began seven years earlier, when Tia, Robertson's middle daughter, began to worry about red spots she detected on her fingertips. Living in New York City at the time, where she worked on Wall Street as a regulator for the National Association of Securities Dealers, the athletic Tia Robertson enjoyed skiing, swimming, golf and tennis. All that would change when, in addition to the spots on her fingertips, she developed a butterfly rash on her face—one of the telltale signs of lupus. Lupus attacks the body's autoimmune system, causing an individual's antibodies to attack vital organs and connective tissue. The disease affects up to two million Americans, most of them women, and it often affects the kidneys, as it did in Tia's case.

Despite treatment for a mild form of the disease, Tia's condition worsened. Her joints began bothering her and, gradually, she began to feel tired and worn down. She stumbled in softball and felt too sore to play tennis. Her parents talked her into moving back home to Cincinnati, where her father offered her a job at one of his three companies. Tia bought a house not far from her parents' home and tried to manage her worsening illness. Oscar said recently, "I looked at her suffering over the years. It hurts. It tears you apart."

DO THE RIGHT THING

Then, in 1994, Tia discovered that she had systemic lupus, the most severe form of the disease. With intensive treatment, her condition remained relatively stable for two years before her renal system began to fail. That decline forced her into kidney dialysis, and she soon found herself hooked up to a kidney machine for seven to eight hours every night. She faced two choices: remain on dialysis for the rest of her life, or undergo a kidney transplant. "I had to start and stop all night," she said of the dialysis. "I really didn't get a lot of sleep. I was ready to have a transplant."

The national waiting list for a kidney contains about 35,000 names. It would be quicker, and more likely successful, if Tia could receive a kidney from a member of her own family. When Tia's father and her sisters underwent testing for compatibility, Tia's older sister, Shana, and Oscar both proved to be prospective donors. But Oscar wouldn't hear of Shana giving up one of her kidneys. "Tia is my daughter," he said, explaining the decision he finally made. "It was my obligation. My wife and I brought her into this world, and it is our responsibility to look after her."

So, on April 10, 1997, Oscar and Tia registered at the hospital under the names Oscar Panama and Tia Paradise. They were wheeled into adjoining rooms, and Oscar's kidney was successfully transplanted to Tia. Their family waited anxiously for the outcome. For Oscar's wife, Yvonne, the wait for news of her husband and daughter was especially difficult. Just months earlier her mother had gone in for a supposedly routine hernia surgery, but had lapsed into a coma from which she never recovered. To Yvonne's relief, Tia and Oscar's surgeries went smoothly. When the team at University Hospital wheeled Tia into her father's room, she simply said, "Thank you for the kidney."

The basketball legend now sports an eighteen-inch scar as a souvenir of his good deed, and one less rib (removed in order for the surgeons to get to Oscar's extraordinarily large kidney). When the press got wind of his selfless act, he responded with characteristic modesty. Robertson had never sought the limelight on the basketball court, so why should he act any differently now? After his daughter's life-saving operation, Robertson revealed a new side to the public. Losing his typical coolness and aloofness, the Basketball Hall of Famer broke into tears as he told the press, "I'm no hero; I'm just a father." Since the operation, he has been surprised by the outpouring of support and affection in the letters and cards he has gotten from people all over the country. Yet, Robertson does not view himself as heroic. When it came time to make things go right, he merely rose to the occasion, as he had so many times in his life.

♣ BUILD TRUST

When my brother Glen Murphy started a business in a small town in North Carolina, he faced the challenge of building trust in a community where cynicism and distrust of business had a long history. Several years ago, Glen decided to invest his life savings in launching a restaurant chain. But where should he locate the new business? And, how could he make it successful? Committed not only to succeeding financially but to doing the right thing, he worked to establish the Murphy Hospitality Corporation in a community where everyone would benefit from the company's presence.

He addressed the location issue by interviewing the directors of industrial development agencies in twenty booming business zones from Raleigh-Durham, North Carolina, to Richmond and Williamsburg, Virginia. As he traveled from city to city, directors greeted him with one success story after another and one business incentive program after another. Still, Glen remained undecided, until he received a unique proposal from a team of business and civic leaders from the town of Warrenton, the seat of North Carolina's poorest county.

Agency directors in Warrenton did not cite success stories or propose attractive incentive programs. Rather, the community offered Glen the opportunity to make a difference by showing distrustful and cynical citizens that a business can do the right thing for a community. The development team promised him he would find tremendous opportunity in Warrenton—as long as he built trust first.

This proposal might not have appealed to the average businessperson, but for one of "Mr. Fantastic's" children, it resonated strongly. It was exactly the type of thing that our father had urged us to pursue. When Glen learned that Warrenton had one of the highest educational drop-out rates in the state—attributed to widespread family instability and lack of incentive for academic pursuits—he saw an opportunity rather than a problem.

Consulting with teachers, administrators and school board members, he proposed an award and recognition program to refocus students and families on the values of a quality education. Borrowing quality-improvement principles from business, particularly those of W. Edwards Demming, Glen led a teacher-community task force in developing a performance-improvement program that would foster a continuous commitment to education and staying in school. It all rested on Glen's willingness to back it up with earnings from his chain of restaurants.

Under the program, at the end of every grading period, teachers would select a student in each class and principals would select one class in each school as having made the most significant contribution to educational self-improvement. As a reward, Glen donated dinner certificates to the winners. He also promoted the program in his restaurants. The educational self-improvement program addressed the community's and schools' central problem: strengthening commitment to the educational process itself, not just to isolated instances of achievement.

It was an ambitious program, especially in light of the fact that its sponsor, Glen's fledgling restaurant franchise operation, had pulled in barely $1,000 in revenue per week during the first several months. But Glen knew that a half-hearted commitment wouldn't build trust. Soon the scope and importance of the program became evident to the whole community, with hundreds of students and classes at all levels eagerly seeking recognition for their scholarly self-improvement.

As the school program gained momentum, other community agencies, including the Warrenton County Family Institute, became involved. Cooperating with that organization to support families in distress, who often needed special emotional assistance, Glen designed a program where families could learn anew how to share good times and solve problems. He used his restaurants to create the haven that many troubled families needed, offering dinner and a table so that families could dine together and work through their problems, often with the guidance of a professional counselor.

As participation in the programs grew, so did trust in the man who put his money behind his principles—and, as the community's trust in Glen Murphy grew, so did its support for the Murphy Hospitality Corporation's franchises. Once the first restaurant became popular and profitable, Glen opened another, and a third is scheduled to open in a renovated historic inn within the next year.

Today, more than 3,000 students and family members per year participate in the educational and family achievement programs Glen launched in his effort to build trust in the Warrenton community. The community, in addition to supporting the Murphy Hospitality Corporation, nominated Glen to receive the Governor's Award for Business Excellence and Volunteer Support. Glen joined representatives from such corporate giants as AT&T and IBM when he accepted the award from the governor. The achievements of Glen and the people of Warrenton show how trust can make what should go right, go right.

♣ SET A PRECEDENT

While Glen Murphy's efforts at improving his community won rather quick recognition, Rachel Carson didn't enjoy such a warm reception when she set about improving the environment. In the 1960s, Carson undertook a daunting task: making known the devastating effect of broad-spectrum pesticides on our environment. In so doing, she challenged a multimillion dollar industry, the political establishment, and public opinion. None of that stopped her because she felt compelled to do what she had to do, when no one else would. She worked tirelessly, even after she learned she had breast cancer, a disease that would eventually prove fatal. The health of the environment, she believed, came before her own health.

Since the pesticide DDT effectively kills mosquitoes, scientists and physicians believed it might help control malaria in the third world, just as, after World War II, it had helped stop the spread of typhus. However, those scientists neglected to consider the fact that DDT also kills robins, trout, grasshoppers and, worst of all, harms children. Rachel Carson did not overlook that fact.

One of America's first woman scientists, Carson graduated from the former Pennsylvania College for Women (now Chatham College) in 1929, and went on to study zoology on scholarship at Johns Hopkins University. She taught zoology at the University of Maryland until she accepted a position as aquatic biologist at the U.S. Bureau of Fisheries, and then at the U.S. Fish and Wildlife Service, where she worked until 1952. Rachel Carson was the first woman to take and pass the civil service test, and one of the few women to hold an upper-level position at the U.S. Fish and Wildlife Service. By the time she left the agency, she had risen in the ranks to become the chief editor of all its publications. In 1952, she won the National Book Award for nonfiction for her book *The Sea Around Us* and decided from then on to dedicate herself full time to writing.

When she worked for the U.S. Fish and Wildlife Service, Carson learned firsthand about the dangers of pesticides. As she further explored the subject, she explained, "It was pleasant to believe... that much of nature was forever beyond the tampering reach of man... the clouds and the rain and the wind were God's." To the contrary, however, her work demonstrated that human tampering could pollute the clouds and the rain and the wind. At first, that realization "was so shocking that I shut my mind—refused to acknowledge what I couldn't help seeing. But that does no good."

If humans could inadvertently harm nature with the pollution that came from modern factories and machinery, Carson wondered, what effect might intentional interference with the balance of nature create? The answer disturbed her deeply. People were, she concluded, slowly but surely destroying their own environment. In 1945 this conclusion compelled her to propose an article on the harmful affects of DDT to *Reader's Digest*. The magazine turned it down. In the winter of 1958, the crisis beckoned Carson again, when pesticides sprayed to control mosquitoes blew across a friend's private bird sanctuary in Massachusetts. So many of her birds died, she sent an angry letter to the *Boston Herald*. She also gave a copy to Carson, along with a note imploring her to convince someone in Washington to look into the problem. "It was in the task of finding that 'someone' that I realized I must write the book," Carson later wrote. The fact was she could find no one willing to investigate. No politician or bureaucrat wanted to rock the boat— big corporations produced DDT and the powerful agricultural industry relied on it heavily.

The very next month, prominent Long Island residents began to insist that the government exclude their land from a gypsy moth eradication campaign involving DDT. Carson wrote to E.B. White, a staff writer for the *New Yorker*, who had shown an interest in preserving American natural resources, to see if he would pick up the story of the Long Islanders' plight. White wrote back, declining to take on the article, but suggesting that Carson consider writing it herself. She did. As she researched the issue and gathered information, a book began to take shape—a brief book, she supposed at first. That book, published as *Silent Spring*, turned into a considerably larger undertaking than she had ever expected.

Carson researched her subject meticulously. It took a lot of time and effort because many sources declined to be identified. In 1960, seeing years' worth of work ahead on the project, she discovered that she had breast cancer. Carson underwent a radical mastectomy, then, with the help of her assistant, continued her work.

In 1962, she finished the book. The *New Yorker* arranged to print excerpts starting in June, and Houghton Mifflin planned to publish the whole thing in September. Even before the *New Yorker* published sections of *Silent Spring*, chemical companies, hearing of Carson's research, waged a campaign to portray pesticides as the modern world's best defense against hunger and disease. Government officials made sexist and personal comments disparaging the integrity of Carson's research and motivations. "I thought she was a spinster," said one, "What's she worried about genetics for?"

However, nothing could stop the book's momentum. Before type was even set to press, the Book of the Month Club rang up advance sales of more than 40,000. Legislators inserted whole sections from the *New Yorker* excerpts into the Congressional Record. When President John F. Kennedy read the book, he ordered the Science Advisory Committee to study the ramifications of pesticide use. For the first time in history, the concept of the "environment" entered the public consciousness.

Rachel Carson succumbed to her cancer two years after the publication of her most famous book. Her influence continues to this day, however. Her endeavors ultimately led to the establishment of the Environmental Protection Agency in 1970. The regulation of pesticides and the administration of the Food Safety Inspection Service come under its jurisdiction, guaranteeing less economically motivated management of these areas.

In 1992, a panel of prominent Americans voted *Silent Spring* the most influential book published in the last fifty years. Carson herself would have dismissed the honor. As she explained before her death, "If I had not written the book, I am sure the ideas would have found another outlet. But knowing the facts as I did, I would not rest until I had brought them to public attention."

Rachel Carson did not rest but took action, using her courage, knowledge and perseverance to take on the business, agricultural and political establishment. By doing the right thing, she made things go right, and she set a precedent for generations of environmentalists who would follow in her footsteps.

❧ GET RESULTS

Like Rachel Carson, Emile Zola challenged public opinion when he involved himself in the infamous Dreyfus affair at the end of the nineteenth century.

An obscure captain in the French army, Alfred Dreyfus came from a Jewish family that had left its native Alsace for Paris when Germany annexed that province in 1871. Dreyfus would likely have served out his stint in the military and then retired into obscurity had not events in a politically unstable France spiraled out of control.

In 1894, secret French documents were discovered in a wastebasket in the office of a German military attaché. Immediately, suspicions arose within the French government that a French military officer was providing secret information to the German government. A multitude of officers, including Captain Dreyfus, could have handled the documents in question, but the investigation settled on Dreyfus, the only Jewish officer with such access.

Army authorities, anxious to regain the trust of the government and public, made up their mind that, evidence or no, Dreyfus was their man. A handwriting expert performed an analysis on the papers found in the German attaché's office, and pronounced Dreyfus' handwriting "similar" to that on the papers. Little other evidence existed, however, and despite his protestations of innocence, a secret military court-martial found Dreyfus guilty of treason. Denied the right to examine the evidence against him, he could not initiate even a feeble defense.

Immediately after his trial, the army stripped Alfred Dreyfus of his rank in a humiliating public ceremony and sentenced him to life imprisonment on Devil's Island, a notorious penal colony off the coast of South America. Enemies of the regime in power took this opportunity to cite Dreyfus' alleged espionage as further evidence of the failures of the Republic. Anti-Semitism, already widespread in France, ran rampant. One newspaper, *La Libre Parole*, declared this incident one among many instances of Jewish treachery.

It appeared that Dreyfus would spend the rest of his life in prison. Few allies supported him, and those who did believe in his innocence felt reluctant to declare their allegiance lest they, too, find themselves accused of treason.

The whole Dreyfus affair might have ended here were it not for a curious and persistent lieutenant colonel who became the new chief of army intelligence two years after Dreyfus' conviction. Lieutenant Colonel Georges Picquart felt no sympathy for the convicted Dreyfus. In fact, he was an uncompromisingly unapologetic anti-Semite. However, he also accepted his duty as an army officer, so when he uncovered evidence that someone had framed Dreyfus, and that the officer who had actually been guilty of espionage still remained on active duty in the army, he did the right thing.

Appalled by the situation, Picquart continued to investigate the affair, ultimately concluding that the guilty officer was a certain Major Walsin Esterhazy. When the lieutenant colonel revealed his findings to army investigators, however, he found them far more interested in covering up a past mistake than in rectifying it. When he persisted in his attempts to reopen the case, the army transferred him to Tunisia. A military court perfunctorily considered the court-martial that Picquart had instigated against Esterhazy; after deliberations that lasted only three minutes, they acquitted him, ignoring the convincing evidence of his guilt.

With Picquart safely shipped out of the country and Dreyfus locked away behind bars, the army higher-ups felt confident that their blunder would remain undetected. They did not count, however, on the righteous intervention of the popular and well-respected writer Emile Zola.

Though not personally involved in the Dreyfus affair at all, Zola was, nevertheless, a fair man who disdained the scathing anti-Semitic attacks issued after the captain's conviction not only at Dreyfus, but at Jews in general. When Zola became aware that, in fact, another individual had committed the treachery blamed on Dreyfus, he chose to make his voice heard, using his celebrity to make the case, so long buried, known to the French people.

Zola published "J'Accuse!," a denunciation of the army cover-up, in the daily newspaper, *L'Aurore*, on January 13, 1898. This open letter to the president of France charged army officers, the minister of war, and the entire war department with framing Dreyfus. He listed each by name, and dared them to sue for libel. On the day the newspaper carried "J'Accuse!," it sold ten times more copies than usual, with the result that the case became an international scandal, and Dreyfus' cause gained credibility both at home and abroad.

After his initial exposé of the Dreyfus scandal, Zola worked unflaggingly for the former army captain's release. He viewed the Dreyfus affair as a disgrace both to the French army, and to the country. As a result of his strongly voiced opinion, Zola found himself accused, tried and convicted of libeling the army. To avoid imprisonment, he fled to England, where he remained until the government eventually granted him amnesty. Even in his exile, however, he continued to speak out in defense of Dreyfus and against the uncontrolled and unreasoned anti-Semitism he so abhorred.

The international attention initiated by Zola forced the French government to look seriously into the affair. The chief of the army's general staff, who had appeared in full dress at Zola's trial to threaten the jury, was replaced. Continuing investigation into the case revealed that the army had suppressed evidence of the captain's innocence. It also found that the espionage for which Dreyfus had been exiled to Devil's Island was still going on. The retired head of the French counter-espionage service tried to notify the president that a Major Esterhazy, not Dreyfus, had actually provided the Germans with the information on troop positions, but the president wanted to hear nothing of this. Dreyfus was tried again during August and early September in 1899, and again found guilty, despite evidence to the contrary. Back he went to Devil's Island.

Later that same year, however, the president, under continued pressure, pardoned Dreyfus, thereby making it possible for him to return to Paris. But the falsely accused Dreyfus had to wait until 1906—twelve years after the case had begun—to be exonerated of the charges and restored to his former military rank.

Although it took time for Zola's outspokenness to get results, his commitment to doing the right thing did eventually reverse a terrible injustice. Risking his reputation, his career, even his life, Zola stood up for what he knew was right. He was, as Anatole France described him at his funeral, "a moment in the conscience of mankind."

♣ DOING RIGHT AND THE NEW MURPHY'S LAW

How easy it seems. Do the right thing. In reality, doing the right thing can require tremendous sacrifice. When you feel tempted to avoid all the hassles that can come along with doing what you know you should do, bear in mind that things do have a tendency to balance themselves out. If you turn your back on an opportunity to make things go right for a relative, a friend, or even a stranger, don't be surprised if, somewhere down the road, someone else takes the same easy path rather than helping you out.

If you want to make doing the right thing more of a habit in your life, think about the lessons revealed by the people profiled in this chapter:

- ♣ **Lesson 1: Value Intangible Rewards.** Kip Keino appreciated and worked to repay the good fortune that came his way by bestowing good fortune on others, not for recognition or gain but for the welfare of those he helped. Do you expect rewards or praise whenever you help someone? Have you ever resented not being properly thanked for a kindness or act of generosity? Do you value the intangible rewards more than the tangible ones you receive? You can't take a trophy or a cash award to your grave, but your reputation and your good deeds will continue to live long after you've gone: prize them more than anything else.

- ♣ **Lesson 2: Protect Your Moral Integrity.** Had Oscar Robertson not given a kidney to his daughter, he would not have been able to live with himself. Have you ever turned away an opportunity to do the right thing then regretted that decision? Do you think more about how performing a good deed will win you the respect of others than how it will win you self-respect? Place a premium on protecting your own moral integrity. Failure to do so could haunt you forever.

- ♣ **Lesson 3: Emphasize Trustworthiness in Your Everyday Activities.** Glen Murphy could have established his business in an affluent community but chose, instead, to locate where he could do the most good by building trust. When making decisions in your day-to-day life, do you try to engender the trust of others? Do you easily place your own trust in others, or do you usually distrust their intentions? When you trust others, they tend to trust you, and when you distrust others, they usually distrust you, too! Let trust guide your actions.

♣ **Lesson 4: Set a Good Precedent**. An individual who does the right thing can, as Rachel Carson's achievements demonstrate, inspire others to do the same. Do you consider the precedent you may be setting when you choose a course of action, or do you act on impulse, regardless of the example you set? Do you consider the precedents set by others when you act, or do you ignore those examples? If people see you doing the right thing, they will feel inspired to do likewise: never forget the influence of each of your daily actions on the behavior of those around you.

♣ **Lesson 5: Let Results Speak Louder Than Words**. Emile Zola wrote and spoke eloquently, but all his eloquence would not have mattered had they not resulted in the right thing happening. Have you ever congratulated yourself on doing the right thing, even if it resulted in no lasting change for the better? Do you measure the results of your actions rather than the actions themselves? Do the right thing, but remain alert to the results. Good intentions and good deeds mean little if they do not bring results for you and those around you.

When you choose to do the right thing, you will find the rewards far outweigh the costs. The most valuable rewards are intangible, but they create tangible results. Moral self-respect, the trust of friends and associates, an exemplary life, and positive results count for more than all the trophies and money in the world.

Rule 9

Give More Than You Receive

"If you haven't any charity in your heart, you have the worst kind of heart trouble."

Bob Hope

♣ GENEROSITY OF HEART

The New Murphy's Law adds a new twist to the old cliché, "'Tis better to give than to receive." Not only does generosity make you feel good, it makes things go right. True benevolence, putting yourself in a position to give to others what you would have them give to you, involves more than a constant generosity of spirit. It means taking action, giving freely of yourself—of your money, of your time, and of your effort—in order to make things go right for others.

When Aaron Feuerstein's company, the Malden Mills, burned to the ground a few years ago, the owner acted in a way that proved he cared more about the welfare of his employees than for his personal profits.

The Malden Mills textile factory in Methuen, Massachusetts was established by Feuerstein's grandfather in 1907. Aaron Feuerstein has lived in New England all of his life and, when he inherited the business, he maintained his loyalty to his community, keeping it in Massachusetts while his competitors abandoned the United States for countries where they could pay employees only a few cents an hour. He knew that the small town of Methuen would turn into a ghost town if he pulled out, taking with him the 2,400 jobs supplied by the Mills.

This loyalty did not come cheap, and Malden Mills suffered serious financial troubles during the early 1980s. Even when the company declared bankruptcy, however, Feuerstein did not give up. Rather, he set about finding a killer idea, a product that would revive Malden Mills' flagging fortunes. His research and development team, which he kept working throughout the financial crisis, did not disappoint him. In the nick of time, they announced that they had developed a lightweight, warm, quick to dry and easy to dye fabric essentially made of recycled plastic. It was the perfect product to compete in the surging fake fur market, which had cut sharply into the demand for Malden Mills' manmade fabrics. Environmentally responsible due to its recycled content, this lightweight, new fabric, "Polartec," appealed to both consumers and clothing manufacturers, especially those who made winter sports apparel. Almost overnight such companies as L.L. Bean, Eastern Mountain Sports, Lands' End, Patagonia and Eddie Bauer were featuring the fabric in their outerwear products and, by 1995, Polartec sales had doubled the revenue for Malden Mills, accounting for half of its $400 million-plus income that year.

It looked like smooth sailing for the company at that point. The townspeople of Methuen felt more secure than ever before, as did Aaron Feuerstein himself. Then everything went terribly wrong, when one night during the winter of 1995, a boiler at the factory exploded, causing a raging fire that injured twenty-seven employees and leveled three of the factory's buildings. The local president of the Union of Needletrades, Industrial and Textile Employees, and also an employee at the Mills, described the catastrophe: "I was standing there seeing the mill burn with my son, who also works there, and he looked at me and said, 'Dad, we just lost our jobs.' Years of our lives seemed gone."

In fact, the livelihood of the entire city seemed doomed. The seventy-year-old Feuerstein would, many assumed, just collect his insurance money and retire. Or, perhaps he would use this turn of events as an excuse to relocate the business overseas. Anyone who thought this, however, didn't really know the man.

Three days after the fire, Feuerstein gathered more than 1,000 people at a local high school gym and announced, "For the next thirty days—and it might be more—all our employees will be paid their full salaries. By January second, we will restart operations, and within ninety days we will be fully operational." No one could believe it—Feuerstein and the Mills were staying! The gym erupted in cheers and hugs.

The company's customers, including L.L. Bean and others, pledged their support. Within days, $330,000 arrived from various companies, the Bank of Boston, the union and a local chamber of commerce. Letters of support, some with modest donations, came from all over the country.

Feuerstein's initial time frame estimates proved overly optimistic. Ninety days came and went, then another ninety, and another. Rebuilding would take much more time and money than he had anticipated. However, this did not weaken Aaron Feuerstein's resolve. True to his word, he kept rebuilding until, in September 1997, the company held its grand reopening, almost two years after the explosion. Incredibly, the Mills rehired 97.4 percent of the workers who had lost their jobs due to the fire. At the opening, Feuerstein expressed his aim of calling the last seventy employees back to work soon. He would not rest easy until he had reunited the entire Malden Mills family.

Despite the tremendous adversity he faced, Aaron Feuerstein consistently maintained his generosity of spirit, acting with resolve on his limitless optimism that he could, and would, make things go right for his community. And his generosity begot generosity, winning him support and loyalty that money can't buy. It moved other companies and other individuals to assist him in his endeavors to keep his business at home and to help the people of Methuen survive in the interim.

Every truly successful person I have met or studied maintains a similar generosity of spirit. Many freely donate their financial resources, but just as many donate their time, lending a sympathetic ear, a helping hand, a word of encouragement. Whatever their occupation or profession, they usually walk one or more of the four paths of generosity:

THE FOUR PATHS OF GENEROSITY

1 One Working for One

2 One Working for Many

3 Many Working for One

4 Many Working for Many

Have you ever given your support, both tangible and intangible, in a one-on-one situation in order to help something go right for another person?

Do you find yourself watching the evening news and thinking, "There are too many problems in the world. I'd like to help, but what can just one person do?" Have you answered that question by doing something that will benefit many other people?

Have you ever seized the opportunity to join forces with others in your organization or neighborhood or community in order to make things better for one needy individual?

Do you ever join with others to help many others?

The individuals and groups profiled in this chapter have moved past mere generosity of spirit to action, behaving in a way that dramatically improved the lives of other people, from those around the corner to those around the world.

♣ ONE WORKING FOR ONE

Few private citizens outside the realm of government have influenced history more than Alfred Nobel. Through his innovations in the explosives and munitions industry, Nobel changed the nature of war but, ironically, through his generosity, he also heightened our awareness of individuals who strive for peace.

Nobel was born in Stockholm, Sweden in 1833, a weak and sickly child who often became so ill that his family and his doctors feared for his life. Nobel's mother, however, never faltered in her devotion to her son; she spent many nights watching wakefully at his bedside, nursing him through crisis after crisis.

While his mother rarely left his side during his early childhood, young Alfred's father rarely appeared in the Nobel household. In 1833, the year of Alfred's birth, Immanuel Nobel went bankrupt. Scrambling to support his still growing family, Immanuel left home for Finland to seek his fortune, and remained absent from his home, and his wife and his three sons, for four years.

When he finally did return, Alfred's father announced that he had indeed found his path to fortune: his invention of an explosive mine. This device had attracted the attention of the czar of Russia, who wanted Immanuel Nobel to manufacture the explosive in the Russian town of St. Petersburg. Thus began the first Nobel munitions factory.

The family moved to Russia, where they lived comfortably from the sales from Immanuel's mines. Immanuel continued to produce invention after invention, building the business to the point that, in 1849, he decided to take his sons out of school and introduce them to the workings of the factory. In 1854, the beginning of the Crimean War flooded the Nobel factory with orders. After that war, however, which proved a disastrous one for Russia, the new czar, Alexander II, canceled all contracts with private enterprises, including the Nobel munitions plant. Soon after, a fire at the main factory sealed the ruin of this once-thriving business. Immanuel Nobel once again went bankrupt.

After their father's business collapsed, each of the Nobel brothers went out on his own. Alfred, who continued working in the field of munitions, began experimenting with a liquid that he had heard about during the Crimean War—nitroglycerin. When he brought the substance to his father's attention, the two began developing a new explosive, and on October 14, 1863 Alfred Nobel recorded his first patent for the resulting nitroglycerin product.

Soon, Nobel began traveling around Europe to promote his fledgling nitroglycerin business. Rapidly developing countries with plans for elaborate railroad lines and extensive mining flocked to purchase this powerful new explosive. Unfortunately, the dangerously unstable liquid required extremely careful handling to prevent its unintended ignition. Inevitably, as the market for the substance spread around the world, accidents began to occur due to leaks or poorly trained workers handling the substance carelessly. After several huge explosions, Nobel began to fear that a widespread panic would cause a ban on the manufacture of his product in some countries. Since he could not possibly prevent the careless handling of nitroglycerin, Nobel decided to find a way to stabilize the substance without reducing its explosiveness.

Nobel set feverishly to work, testing a number of substances for their ability to absorb his nitroglycerin, including sawdust, brick dust, charcoal, and cement. The answer to Nobel's problem, though, came not through his experimentation, but by sheer luck. In one of his shipments, someone had replaced the sawdust padding around the nitroglycerin with clay. When one can in the crate leaked, Nobel noticed that the clay soaked up all of the liquid, but still remained granular. Tests on this material in his lab showed that it reacted to heat and to shock in the same way as nitroglycerin. When he detonated it with a percussion cap, he witnessed an explosion even more powerful than that achieved with straight nitroglycerin. Nobel patented the substance under two names: "Nobel's Safety Powder" and "Dynamite." His business boomed, with new dynamite factories springing up all around Europe.

At the age of forty-three, Alfred Nobel now enjoyed the life of a very wealthy man. He took up full-time residence in Paris and hired a personal secretary to oversee his affairs. This woman, Bertha von Suttner, would bring to bear a profound influence on her boss and, through him, on the world.

Bertha was a beautiful and poised woman of thirty-three, a descendent of nobility who still bore the title of Countess Bertha Kinsky von Chinic und Tettau. Bertha's mother, however, had gambled away the family fortune and left her daughter to fend for herself. Thus, the Countess went to work as a secretary.

Nobel, deeply touched by Bertha's plight and impressed by her intelligence, wit and integrity, quickly developed a warm and lasting friendship with her. Even after Bertha married and left Alfred's employ, their association continued. Then, around the turn of the century, Bertha and her husband, who had been spending most of their time in the Caucuses, paid a visit to Alfred Nobel in Paris. Europe was already enmeshed in the unrest that would ultimately result in the first world war, and the talk in Paris centered around this topic. Bertha announced to Nobel her decision to wage a fight for peace. She questioned his continued involvement in the munitions field and attempted to persuade him to join her cause.

Nobel had long believed that continued experimentation in weaponry and munitions would, through the creation of a weapon "of such horrible capacity for mass annihilation," make the waging of war impossible. He believed that the potential for mass destruction would, in fact, forestall any future aggression. The combination, however, of the persistent whispering of impending war and Bertha's insistent pleading began to alter Alfred Nobel's point of view.

Bertha waged her war for peace through the writing of a novel, *Die Waffen Nieder!* (*Lay Down Your Arms!*). The book became quite popular in Europe, and it won Bertha an invitation to attend the Third World Peace Conference as chairman of the Austrian delegation. By the time the Fourth Conference convened in Berne, Switzerland, Bertha had convinced Nobel to attend. When the two parted company after the conference,

GIVE MORE THAN YOU RECEIVE

Nobel pledged to do something great for the peace movement. Realizing that contrary to his former beliefs, his life's work had probably not led the world away from war, he vowed that he would use his great wealth to reward an individual who had done so.

On January 7, 1893, Alfred Nobel wrote to Bertha: "I should like to allot part of my fortune to the formation of a prize fund to be distributed in every period of five years… this prize would be awarded to the man or woman who had done the most to advance the idea of general peace in Europe...." This generous donation would come to be known as the Nobel Peace Prize. Two years after he wrote this letter, in November 1895, Alfred Nobel signed his final will, including the permanent establishment of the prize, which he insisted should go to "the person who has done the most effective work to promote friendship between nations, and to secure the elimination or reduction of standing armies...."

During the year that he drafted his last will, Nobel moved back to Sweden, and a year later, on December 10, 1896, he died. The first Nobel Peace Prize, awarded exactly five years after his death, went to Henri Dunant of Switzerland, who founded the Red Cross, and to Fredric Passy, a renowned French pacifist. Subsequently, other Nobel prizes were created to expand the effort and utilize the fortune Nobel had bequeathed for the prize.

Today, we remember Alfred Nobel more for the Peace Prize he established than for the dynamite he invented. Each year when the Nobel Prize Committee announces the name of a person who has tried to make the world a better, more peaceful place, that individual receives both a financial reward and worldwide publicity for his or her cause. As a summary of his life's work, Nobel chose the course of generosity and personally sought to recognize those individuals whose singular contributions make things go right for all of us.

♣ ONE WORKING FOR MANY

If you saw such celebrities as Dustin Hoffman, Gregory Peck, Lily Tomlin, Leslie Caron, and Whoopi Goldberg gathered together in one place, what kind of event would you think you had happened upon? An Oscar party or a movie premiere perhaps? Believe it or not, you could actually be witnessing not a glamorous Hollywood party, but something much more meaningful. These celebrities, and many more, form the advisory board for the Audrey Hepburn Hollywood for Children Fund (HFC).

Audrey Hepburn was born in Brussels, Belgium, in 1929, the multilingual and cosmopolitan daughter of a Dutch Baroness and an English banker. During the 1930s she lived in England, Belgium and the Netherlands, where she spent many of her teen years during the Nazi occupation of World War II. Although just a youngster, Audrey Hepburn demonstrated her generosity and kindness by volunteering to raise funds for the Dutch Resistance. A devotee of dance, she performed in underground concerts, dedicating the proceeds to support the Resistance fighters. In addition to raising money, she also risked her life for the cause, acting as a courier to deliver messages. Life in wartime Holland was, of course, grueling and difficult. The lack of food and general hardships she faced during the occupation left the young Hepburn with an altered metabolism, the rumored cause of the actress's legendary slimness.

On Audrey Hepburn's sixteenth birthday, the Allies liberated the Netherlands. Hepburn always remembered the welcome sight of the International Red Cross and United Nations workers who stepped forward to provide desperately needed food and medical care to the beleaguered Dutch.

After the war, Hepburn moved to the South of France, where she worked as a model and bit-part actress to finance her dance studies. Her career took off when the renowned French playwright, Colette, offered her the title role in the Broadway version of *Gigi*. Both the show and its star were a smashing success. After this American debut, the engaging young actress landed the lead role in *Roman Holiday*, starring opposite Gregory Peck. Her work in this 1953 film earned Hepburn an Oscar for Best Actress as well as international fame.

From that point on, Hepburn's career soared. She performed in films that many critics consider eternal classics, such as *Sabrina*, *Breakfast at Tiffany's* and *My Fair Lady*. Audrey Hepburn did not let her success go to her head; in fact, the modest celebrity said, "I probably hold the distinction of being one movie star who, by all the laws of logic, should never have made it. At each stage of my career, I lacked the experience." Hepburn felt forever grateful for the praise showered upon her by filmmakers and by the public. Even after her tremendous success, she also remained ever mindful and appreciative of the invaluable aid she had received from the volunteers who had served her and thousands of others at the end of World War II.

Audrey Hepburn determined to try to repay the kindness that the Red Cross and the United Nations workers had shown. Throughout most of her career, she made a point of using her high profile to draw attention to worthy charities. During the last five years of her life, in particular, she committed herself to the plight of the world's forgotten children, serving as a Goodwill Ambassador for UNICEF, and traveling tirelessly around the world to Ethiopia, Central and South America, Bangladesh, the Sudan and Vietnam. The suffering of the innocent children she encountered throughout her travels appalled her so much that she grew determined to expand her humanitarian work, even though she began to suffer terrible abdominal pains during her travels. Despite her doctor's persistent warnings, Hepburn kept working for her cause, setting aside her own pain in order to relieve the pain of suffering children.

Later, she learned that she was in fact suffering from colon cancer. On Wednesday, January 20, 1993, shortly after her diagnosis, Audrey Hepburn passed away at her home in Tolochenez, Switzerland, surrounded by family and friends.

Upon her death, UNICEF Executive Director James P. Grant said, "Audrey was unique: as a movie star and as a UNICEF Goodwill Ambassador. Moved by a profound love of children, she repeatedly set aside the comforts of home to visit some of the most deprived and often forgotten people of this planet, for whom she became an effective voice. Her eloquent and deeply moving appeals on their behalf helped raise not only funds but the conscience of the world community."

So that the good works that Audrey Hepburn steadfastly performed should not cease after her death, her son, Sean Ferrer, along with numerous other friends and family members, founded the Audrey Hepburn Hollywood for Children Fund. This organization has brought together dozens of celebrities, all bent on continuing in Hepburn's footsteps, extending the star's legacy of helping children in need all over the world.

One woman did so much for so many. Audrey Hepburn translated her own gratitude into generosity, and by doing so prompted many others to do the same. Every hour she dedicated to helping needy children will be multiplied hundreds of times over by the renewed enthusiasm for giving that her actions inspired.

☘ MANY WORKING FOR ONE

Who among us has not been moved at witnessing the devastation wreaked on survivors of a natural disaster? Floods along the Mississippi delta, hurricanes in Florida, earthquakes in California—all such catastrophes have tested the mettle of those who endured them, and the generosity of those who rush to their aid.

As a nation, we Americans do rush to the aid of communities in such dire straits, but how often do we do the same for just one individual who has suffered a personal tragedy? San Diego Chargers' owner Alex Spanos and the corps of volunteers he inspired did just that.

Alex Spanos has long made a habit of giving—and giving generously—to society. The son of Greek immigrants from Kalamata, Spanos did not come into this world with a silver spoon in his mouth. He did become rich, but he worked hard for every dime, founding the A.G. Spanos Construction Company in 1960, then building his business and his fortune from scratch. His hard work paid off, and today his company is one of the largest builders of apartment buildings in the United States. His business success allowed him to fulfill a life-long dream when, in 1984, the opportunity arose for him to buy the San Diego Chargers football franchise.

Despite the fact that hard work, not legacy or luck, has brought about his good fortune, Spanos feels a responsibility to help others as a means of thanking society for his good fortune. Spanos' generosity has touched countless lives through his charitable, civic, athletic, religious, artistic and educational contributions. He has donated liberally to numerous charities, including the United Service Organization, the YMCA, the Red Cross, and many children's organizations such as the Children's Hospital and Health Center in San Diego.

He has responded, like many of us, to the huge national disasters, at one point donating one million dollars to assist flood victims in California.

All of this, of course, makes Alex Spanos a remarkable and admirable man. However, his true benevolence shines most brilliantly from a less well-known contribution to one woman—stranded, alone, and in trouble—a contribution that inspired an entire community to come together to help that individual.

Kharen Pella came from Spanos' hometown of Stockton, California, but was working as a volunteer halfway around the world when tragedy struck. A teacher at the International Cambodian School of Phnom Penh, she was badly burned in an accident on February 6, 1996. She survived the accident and entered the Visal Sok Hospital in Cambodia for treatment. However, Pella's problems did not end with her injury; she had no health insurance to pay for her care, and she could not even afford to come home.

Pella languished, stranded in Cambodia for two months. On April 3, an article appeared in a local Stockton paper describing the plight of the teacher. Immediately upon hearing of Pella's situation, Alex Spanos stepped forward to offer the use of his private plane to bring her home.

When word of Spanos' generosity circulated in Stockton, local residents volunteered in droves to assist in the cause, donating more than $35,000 to help pay for Pella's medical care. Ten people, out of numerous volunteers, made the long and difficult journey to Cambodia in order to accompany and care for the injured teacher during her trip.

Spanos' jet, a Gulf Stream III, left Stockton at seven o'clock in the morning on April 16. It made stops in Alaska, Japan, and China, before finally landing at its destination of Phnom Penh. After Pella joyfully boarded the plane, the volunteers did what they could to make her comfortable on the return flight. They once again stopped in Osaka and in Anchorage before reaching San Francisco International Airport at three in the afternoon on April 18. The hardy volunteers had traveled 14,226 miles in only two and a half days.

Alex Spanos went to the airport to welcome Pella home. "You shouldn't have to worry about anything," he assured her, "Just take care of yourself."

Kharen Pella immediately began to do just that. Paramedics donated by the Stockton branch of the American Medical Response ambulance company transported her from the airport to San Francisco General Hospital, where she was reunited with her family—her four children and her brother.

Pella's relatives were overwhelmed by the amazing effort made by so many on behalf of their loved one. Pella's oldest daughter, Nhicolle Clayton, exclaimed, "I want to thank the community. I want to thank Mr. Spanos. Hopefully in our lives we can turn around and do something for somebody in the same way." Alex Spanos, through his generosity toward one individual in need, inspired a spiral of benevolence that made things go right.

♣ MANY WORKING FOR MANY

When William and Kathy Magee traveled to the Philippines in 1981 as substitute volunteers on a five-day long medical mission to help repair the health and self-esteem of children suffering from cleft lips and cleft palates, they did not imagine that this brief sojourn would alter their lives forever.

Before accompanying a team of American doctors on this mission, the Magees enjoyed a comfortable suburban life in Norfolk, Virginia. They were a fairly typical American couple: high school sweethearts who wed in 1967, a few years after each had graduated from college. They worked hard to create a good life for themselves and for the family they hoped to create. At first, Kathy worked as a pediatric nurse while William completed dental school. After William graduated, he practiced dentistry at night so that he could attend medical school during the day. After receiving his M.D. and doing internships both in the United States and abroad, William Magee established his reconstructive plastic surgery practice in Virginia.

In December 1981, when the call came inviting the couple to journey to the Philippines with a team of plastic surgeons, they were the parents of five children, ranging in age from six to thirteen years old. Although making arrangements for the care of their large family posed a daunting problem, the Magees' desire to be of service overcame any doubts. They arranged for the care of their four youngest, and took their oldest daughter, Brigette, along as an assistant.

The situation that greeted the Magees in the Philippines agonized them. Hundreds of children suffering from grotesque deformities, many potentially life-threatening, clamored for the services of the volunteer surgeons. Their deformities had made social outcasts of many of these children. Even worse than the social stigma, however, the cleft lips and palates made it difficult for these children to speak, attend school, and sometimes even to eat. "Everywhere we turned, there was a sea of deformities," reflected Kathy Magee. "People pushed their babies at us, tugged at our sleeves with tears in their eyes and begged us to help their children."

The team visited three cities in five days, completing an astounding 150 operations. Heartbreakingly, though, the surgeons had to turn away another 250 children in desperate need of help. The Magees, unwilling to leave their work in the Philippines unfinished, vowed to return as soon as they could in order to help those who had been turned away this time. "I couldn't bear looking at these faces and having to say I was sorry," said Dr. Magee.

Immediately upon returning to Norfolk, the Magees launched into a fevered grassroots fundraising endeavor aimed at financing their return mission to the Philippines. They arranged pot luck dinners and held Bingo games, and they recruited the volunteer services of eighteen additional doctors, nurses and technicians to the project they dubbed Operation Smile. On their return mission, the Magees and their team provided surgical care to 200 more children. After this second trip, the couple decided that Operation Smile must become a permanent organization.

Since that second mission in 1982, Operation Smile's programs have grown and expanded. It began with the small group of friends who returned with the Magees to the Philippines, and today Operation Smile's volunteer army has burgeoned to 28,000 members. In addition to the Philippines, these volunteers serve seventeen other countries, including Russia, Colombia, Brazil, Vietnam, China, Romania, Morocco and the United States. The need in developing countries particularly concerns the Magees, where the rate of deformity can run as high as one in 500, more than double the rate in the United States.

The generosity of William and Kathy Magee's army has changed the lives of over 43,000 suffering children. In addition to treating cleft lips and palates, surgeons have removed tumors, corrected extreme hand deformities, treated burn damage and facial nerve damage, among other serious problems. They have never charged a dime for their services.

In addition to the surgeries they have performed, Operation Smile has instituted physician training programs in their mission countries, wherein they teach local doctors the specialized surgical skills used by their volunteers. Local physicians receive free training with the understanding that they will continue the benevolent work of Operation Smile by treating at least one physically deformed child per week for free. In this way, the good work of Operation Smile can serve a community long after the volunteers have departed.

William and Kathy Magee have parlayed a personal commitment into an international organization that has immeasurably benefited thousands upon thousands. In 1999, they plan to launch a new program, "The Smile Train," which will allow them to treat more than seven times as many needy children as they can currently serve. As Dr. Magee has said, "What began as an idea to help only a few children has grown into a network of volunteers and medical missions transforming thousands of lives... and the progression of smiles across the world is growing."

♣ GENEROSITY
AND THE NEW MURPHY'S LAW

The people you have met in this chapter demonstrate the power of generosity. Whether one person helps one other person, one helps many, many help one, or many help many, the act of giving more than you receive makes things go right.

To tap that power yourself, keep these lessons in mind:

♣ **Lesson 1: Self-Interest and Compassion Coexist.** Aaron Feuerstein demonstrated that self-interest and compassion can coexist. Have you made a commitment to become an active member of your own community? Do you carefully consider the welfare of those around you before making your own decisions? If you feel that your own actions can do little to affect your community, remember the difference just one generous person can make in the world.

♣ **Lesson 2: There Is Never a Wrong Time to Begin Listening to Your Conscience.** Alfred Nobel lived most of his life believing that his munitions manufacturing would help the cause of peace; not until the end of his life did he see the error in his thinking. When he did, he chose to recognize one person's efforts toward peace. Do you engage in one-on-one relationships where you give as much, or more, than you receive? Have you ever expected more from someone else than you were willing to give that person? All generosity begins one-on-one: look for opportunities to act on your generosity toward one other person.

♣ **Lesson 3: Return Kindness with Kindness.** Audrey Hepburn never forgot the kindness of the volunteers who came to her aid in war-torn Holland. Have you ever found yourself taking for granted the acts of kindness you receive? Do you make it a practice to show your appreciation when someone goes out of his or her way to lend you a helping hand? By observing the rule that one good turn deserves another, you will advance the process of reciprocity in which kindness begets kindness.

♣ **Lesson 4: Motivate Generosity in Others with Your Own Generosity.** As the story of Alex Spanos aptly illustrates, one person can inspire many people to aid one individual. Do you look for individuals with whom you work or live who may need more assistance than you can provide yourself? Do you accept invitations to join others in helping out one needy person? Join hands with others, help one person, and watch that one person return the favor by helping others.

♣ **Lesson 5: Create a Spiral of Generosity.** William and Kathy Magee and those and those involved in Operation Smile apply their medical training to improve the lives of countless others. Do you look for ways to band together with others to improve the lives of many in need? Have you supported or worked for an organization that reaches out nationally or internationally to those in need? No matter what your own individual talents, some organization can put those to use helping others: participate regularly, if only part-time, in such an effort.

Generosity. It begins in the heart, it begins at home, but it casts a pebble in a pond that can keep on creating ripples long after the act itself.

Rule 10

Never, Never, Never Give Up

"You're never a loser until you quit trying."

Mike Ditka

♣ "THE ENVELOPE, PLEASE."

We begin our journey with hope and optimism, we follow the rules of the road that enable us to make things go right, but as we travel we can't avoid all the setbacks, potholes, detours and roadblocks that get between us and our dreams. The New Murphy's Law does not make those obstacles disappear, but it does give us the persistence and perseverance to overcome whatever gets in our way. We New Murphys never, never, *never* give up.

Few roads to success pose more obstacles than the one that leads to fame and fortune in Hollywood. Every day another young would-be star steps off a bus onto the star-studded streets ready to conquer the entertainment world. For the hopeful actor or actress, the warnings of concerned parents go unheeded and the knowledge of the overwhelming odds against success get pushed to the back of the mind. The aspiring star keeps thinking, "People get discovered all the time, why not me?" Indeed, with great perseverance, some do achieve stardom—the kind that Matt Damon and Ben Affleck achieved in 1997.

The pair met as children in South Boston when Matt was just ten years old and Ben only eight. Ben had already achieved a bit of celebrity, doing some television work on a PBS series. His new friend Matt shared his dream of performing, and the two became fast friends. The two boys often acted in plays together, even staging a few of their own. By the time they reached high school, they had begun to hatch their plans to take Hollywood by storm.

As youngsters, the duo's attempts to "break into the business" sometimes ended in misadventure. On one particular occasion, Ben set up an audition at Disney in New York through the agent he had worked with as a boy. He and Matt bragged to their friends that they were heading to the Big Apple to meet with the president of Disney Studios. Much to their surprise, they arrived, confident of their imminent success, only to find out that they would be auditioning for the *Mouseketeers*— not exactly the glory roles they had envisioned.

After high school, when college and nine-to-five jobs failed to suit them, the two finally elected to make the trip to Hollywood. Despite the enormous odds against them, both Matt and Ben tirelessly studied acting and auditioned for roles. With each minor screen appearance they slowly gathered experience, but invariably they would finish the assignment only to return to obscurity. Each accumulated a small list of mostly for-gettable screen credits, which they desperately tried to parlay into future work. In 1992, they shared the screen in the film, *School Ties*. However, the more heralded young actors in the movie, Chris O'Donnell and Brendan Fraser, received most of the limelight after its release.

Matt and Ben shared a small apartment in Los Angeles, which served as home base for several years. Audition after audition, rejection after rejection, they pressed onward, at last reaching the moment of truth that faces all hungry young actors: should they pack it all in and go back to Boston? Their dingy apartment and pasta meals had grown tiresome, and the rejections had become numbing. However, while other strug-gling actors were boarding the bus back home, these two young dynamos reached a climactic decision: if no one would cast them, they would cast themselves. They decided to resurrect a forty-page, one-act play that Matt had begun to write for an English class a few years back. In 1992, the two actors determined to turn this fragment into their own full-length screenplay.

The story focused on a character named Will, a math prodigy from a broken home and a bad neighborhood who had never made use of his talents. The setting was the streets of South Boston, where the pair had grown up, and the characters were loosely based on people they had known. Matt would play Will, and Ben would play a supporting part as Will's best friend. The two worked hard at writing dialogue that delved into the most basic human emotions, words that an audience would find believable and compelling.

Matt and Ben worked sporadically over the course of five years to better define and develop these charac-ters, setting the screenplay aside periodically for small scraps of work that came their way. Then, the unex-pected happened: their acting careers slowly began to take off. As with most of their endeavors, their success came simultaneously. In 1996, Affleck landed the lead role in Kevin Smith's third film, *Chasing Amy*, and Damon played Rudy Baylor in Francis Ford Coppola's *The Rainmaker*. Suddenly, they found themselves closer to the success they had been pursuing.

By this time, Damon's agent had agreed to read their script, *Good Will Hunting*. The agent liked it enough to pass it along to a literary agent. Within days, a bidding war ensued involving several studios. The pair anxiously waited by the telephone—and, after what seemed an eternity, the calls finally came. Studios liked the story and wanted to buy it, but they wanted to cast high-profile stars in key roles rather than the writers. The two had waited, worked, and struggled for so long that, for a seven-figure paycheck, they felt tempted to acquiesce. But they talked it out and decided that, rather than give in, they would stick to their guns. They would play the parts or there would be no deal.

At last, Miramax films offered a half-million dollars for the script, a lower price than other offers, but one that included casting Matt and Ben. Equally important to the two scriptwriters, Miramax agreed to shoot the film in South Boston, rather than in a less expensive location such as Toronto.

Few stories of perseverance end more euphorically than this one. In March of 1998, Matt and Ben won the Academy Award for Best Original Screenplay for *Good Will Hunting*, which they accepted to a standing ovation from the very people who would not return their phone calls a year before. Their boyish enthusiasm turned to elation on stage, serving as a reminder to the jaded Hollywood community that making movies should be, more than anything, a lot of fun. And, it reminded the rest of us that no matter how far off our dreams appear, we must never give up trying to reach them.

Of course we cannot all become movie stars, but we can employ the same determination and ambition that drove Matt Damon and Ben Affleck. Whether you are trying to learn to play the piano or to play chess, whether you hope to climb Mount Everest or climb the corporate ladder, persistence and tenacity are rewarded.

FOUR REWARDS OF PERSISTENCE

1   Personal Achievement

2   Financial Security

3   Personal Influence

4   Historical Impact

Did you ever nurture a daydream that you vowed one day would come true? If so, have you ever abandoned it in the face of harsh reality?

Do you cultivate a special talent that might someday earn you a fortune?

Have you ever believed in a cause so firmly that you were willing to fight for it indefinitely?

Can you face up to seemingly overwhelming opposition without faltering? Do you think about the impact your perseverance will have on others?

The people in this chapter have posed such questions to themselves—and have answered them with confidence and determination.

♣ PERSONAL ACHIEVEMENT

Some people, blessed with quick minds and photographic memories, seem to succeed in school with no effort. Quick feet and strong hands enable others to excel on the athletic field. Colleges and universities vie for both types each fall, hoping to attract the best scholars and the best athletes to their campuses. What happens, though, to a young man who dreams of going to a great school and playing for its celebrated football team, but lacks both the academic and athletic prowess to make it happen? If he's Daniel "Rudy" Ruettiger Jr., he doesn't let that stop him.

Growing up as the third of fourteen children, everyone told Rudy that he was too small and too slow to amount to much of anything. Sometimes that message came from his own insensitive brothers, other times from friends or teachers. Meanwhile, his millworker father taught Rudy to worship the Notre Dame football team of the 1960s. In their little blue-collar town of Joliet, Illinois, the exploits of the Fighting Irish offered a momentary escape from the daily grind. Fantasizing, as most kids do, Rudy pictured himself on the field in the trademark gold helmet, adding to the gridiron legend. Each year, though, his small stature and poor grades made that dream more and more unlikely. Still, playing football for Notre Dame gradually became an obsession for Rudy Ruettiger.

Upon graduating high school, Ruettiger grudgingly did what everyone, especially his family, expected him to do: work in the mill. For four years, he toiled away with his brothers and his best friend, Pete, close by, all living the same monotonous life. One fateful day, an accident in the mill claimed Pete's life and, paradoxically, marked the beginning of Rudy's. After denying his dream for years, Pete's death made Rudy realize how swiftly life can pass by.

So, against the wishes of his family and his girlfriend, Rudy took the thousand dollars he had saved from his job at the mill and boarded a bus to South Bend, Indiana, home of the Fighting Irish. At the age of twenty-two, Rudy Ruettiger was going to get into Notre Dame or die trying. Unfortunately, he did not have a clue about how to do it. After riding the bus all night to the legendary campus, he wound up on the doorstep of one of the university's priests. For once, fate intervened on Rudy's behalf; after hearing Rudy's story, the man took pity on him and offered to help him get into Holy Cross, a junior college down the road. The priest told Rudy that if he could manage to improve his grades there, he might possibly qualify to transfer to Notre Dame. As for playing football, the good father told Rudy that would require more help than a mere mortal could supply.

Rudy wasted no time. He enrolled in Holy Cross and, within a few days, knocked on the door of Notre Dame's football coach, Ara Parseghian, proclaiming his intentions to play for him. Rudy's sincere but preposterous announcement prompted the same expression of disbelief that he had received all his life. Still, the young man's determination impressed Parseghian. The coach offered Rudy a position—not on the football field, but on the maintenance crew.

For the next several months, Rudy studied diligently at Holy Cross with the help of a tutor, did his work on the Notre Dame football field, built up his muscles with strenuous workouts, and spent Saturday afternoons watching games from the bleachers. While he waited for his moment to come, he lived rent-free in a storage room at the field, sleeping on a cot.

His first report card from Holy Cross rewarded his labor; Rudy had earned two As and three Bs. To be sure, Holy Cross did not quite match Notre Dame in terms of academic rigor, but this hint of success shored up his confidence, giving him the impetus to continue striving toward his dream. Each semester, Rudy continued to hit the books with fervor, always cognizant of the fact that unless he could gain admission to Notre Dame as a full-fledged student, he would never play football there.

Dazed with anticipation, he tore open the reply to his first application for transfer to Notre Dame, only to learn that he had been denied. The frustration did not undermine his determination one iota. Instead, he studied harder and pumped more iron. Again, he submitted his application for acceptance, and again he was turned away. After two years of dedication to a school that would not admit him, Rudy finally faced his last chance. The school did not accept senior transfers, so the next response would seal his fate. Imagine the tears of joy that burst from the eyes of the driven dynamo as he read the word, "Congratulations." Now he could concentrate on the second half of his dream.

Again, Rudy wasted no time. Knowing that Notre Dame still conducted walk-on tryouts for its football team, he resolved to impress the coaches there. A whirling dervish, he flew all over the field, making hits and diving after footballs. When practice concluded, the coaches conferred. Unanimously, they agreed that he had shown more guts than any other candidate, even though he displayed very little talent for the game. One coach suggested that they give him a chance to suit up on the practice squad, meaning he would practice against the team during the week, but would not suit up for games. Rudy didn't care—he had made the team.

Week after week, Rudy dutifully showed up at practice, sacrificing his body for the greater glory of the Fighting Irish. By the middle of Rudy's senior year, his teammates had come to admire his unflinching commitment and wished he could dress for a real game almost as badly as he did. But that seemed only a pipe dream.

The last Saturday of the season rolled around. It was Rudy's last chance. When he read the list of players who would take the field during this last game, however, he saw that his name was not on it. The disappointment cut through him so sharply that, for the first time in his life, he wanted to quit.

Then, the spirit that he had brought to the Notre Dame locker room moved his teammates to lobby the coach to let him play, a request Parseghian grudgingly agreed to honor. On a fall day in 1975, Rudy Ruettiger put on a game uniform for the first and last time as a player for the Fighting Irish. His father watched from the stands as Rudy's teammates took a commanding lead in the game. As the clock wound down, the team and the crowd began to chant "Rudy! Rudy! Rudy!" His name would not go down in the record book unless he participated in the game, and everybody knew it. With twenty-seven seconds to go in the game, the season, and Rudy's football career at Notre Dame, the coach gave Rudy the thumbs up. Miraculously, on the very next play Rudy shot through a gap in the line and sacked the quarterback with a lifetime's worth of pent-up enthusiasm. When the game ended, Rudy left the stadium on his teammates' shoulders, an unlikely but inspiring football hero.

After earning his degree from Notre Dame, Rudy went on to turn his incredible story into a motivational speaking career. TriStar Pictures made a movie in 1993 chronicling his life, and he later published a book called *Rudy's Rules: How to Reach Your* Dreams (Rudy Int'l, 1994). Without question, Rudy Ruettiger offers hope to anyone who fears that he or she lacks the natural gifts needed to succeed in any chosen field of endeavor: things can go right if you never, ever give up.

♣ FINANCIAL SECURITY

Beatrix Potter was born on July 28, 1866, in the London district of Kensington to a well-to-do family, where she grew up surrounded by servants. Her parents raised her and her younger brother, Bertram, according to the strict child-rearing regimens of Victorian England, spending little time with the children themselves.

Young Beatrix and Bertram found their lives full of regimentation. Not even their annual holiday brought much relief from the daily routine, but it did provide a change of scenery for the children, and a bit more opportunity to explore the natural world around them in the countryside. At Dalguise House in Scotland, where they stayed every summer, the children would take walks alone and spend long days sketching the plants and animals they saw.

During these adventures, Beatrix and Bertram often caught rabbits, frogs and other small creatures to keep as pets. Their tiny menagerie would travel back to London with them in cages. If a pet died, Beatrix and Bertram would sometimes skin the body, boil it down to the bones, and reconstruct its skeleton. Far from a gruesome hobby, this careful study of anatomy lent incredible realism to the youthful Potters' sketches.

When the time came for Bertram to go off to boarding school, Beatrix found her life in London even more constricted, dividing her time between lessons from a governess and lonely hours in her room on the third floor of the family's house.

Naturally, the quiet little girl devoted herself to her sketch work and to her many pets, an ever-changing collection of hedgehogs, mice, rabbits, frogs, and snakes. She kept the creatures warm and well fed. When they slept, she sketched her tiny models incessantly.

Before long, Beatrix begged her parents for art lessons. Fortunately, the older Potters loved art themselves, and counted among their friends the painter James Whistler, whose *Study in Black and Grey* has become famous under its nickname, "Whistler's Mother." They granted Beatrix her wish.

Her art lessons become almost her only escape from home. By the time she reached adolescence, she gradually came to realize that her parents expected her eventually to take over running the household for them. She accepted this with a certain sense of resignation, but as time went on, she would yearn ever more passionately for her freedom.

Art would, it turned out, open the door to that freedom when Beatrix wrote and illustrated a little story for her friend Annie Moore's children. The story was *The Tale of Peter Rabbit*. The Moore children so loved the story that they implored Potter to send them more. And so began the career of one of literature's most successful children's book authors. Given the restrictions in her life and the limited opportunities afforded women in those days, pursuing that career took more than a little perseverance.

Resolving to see the Peter Rabbit story in print, Potter took the manuscripts and detailed drawings to publisher after publisher, only to come away with rejection after rejection. One publisher disdainfully commented that the tale "smelled like rotting carrots." Another agreed to publish the book if Potter would make it larger and more colorful, but the author refused the offer because she wanted a book small enough for "little hands" and feared that color illustrations would make the book too expensive for many families.

Finally, in 1902, she decided to self-publish the book just the way she envisioned it, using as funding a gift from her father and the little money she had earned illustrating greeting cards. After distributing this edition among family and friends, she decided that although Frederick Warne and Company publishers had turned her down earlier, she would submit the finished product yet again. The company had a tradition of publishing affordable, high-quality books, and its editors saw potential in Potter's *The Tale of Peter Rabbit*. They quickly agreed to publish it, promising that although they would use color illustrations, they would still make the book affordable.

Even as Potter edited Peter Rabbit's story, she began work on a new book, *The Tailor of Gloucester*. Again she printed an edition for family and friends, but when Warne requested another book, she agreed to edit *The Tailor of Gloucester* for widespread publication. For the next ten years the Warne publishing company released one or two Potter books a year. The books sold so well that they made the author an independently wealthy woman. Through her perseverance, Beatrix Potter finally gained the freedom she so ardently desired.

Her first big purchase with her newfound wealth was a farm in England's Lake District—which was not only a good investment, as she explained to her parents, but, finally, a place of her own. Although she remained dutiful to her parents and made herself available to them when they really needed her, she managed to spend a lot of time at this long-yearned-for retreat. By not giving up on her dream, Beatrix Potter gained financial independence and made things go right in her life.

♣ PERSONAL INFLUENCE

Breakthroughs in cancer research have been making headlines lately, and each of them proves the power of perseverance. Virtually every medical researcher working on the frontier of science owes a debt to Dr. Jonas Salk, whose determination never wavered as he sought a cure for polio.

In 1916 a devastating disease began its reign of terror in the United States. Polio, known as "The Crippler," was a silent predator: no one knew how it spread, and no one knew how to stop it. Each year, when summer vacation started, The Crippler swung into action. Baffled and terrified parents refused to let their children swim, play in parks, drink from water fountains, or even go to movie theaters, lest they fall victim to the dreaded disease.

Their fears were warranted. From seemingly nowhere the illness would strike. One morning, a child would complain of a fever and cramps, and parents' hearts would break. Of the lucky children who lived, many remained confined to iron lungs (immobilizing contraptions the size of a subcompact car), wheelchairs, braces, or years of rehabilitation. Polio "was the AIDS of the 50s," *Life* magazine said in 1990, "And then... one man delivered us."

That man was Jonas Salk. Dr. Salk's path to his discovery was marked by determination, stubbornness, and the ambition to do something good for humanity— "to be of some help to humankind... in a larger sense than just on a one-to-one basis."

Born in New York City in 1914, Salk was the oldest of three sons of Russian-Jewish immigrants. His mother received no formal schooling, and his father, a garment worker, only finished elementary school. Both, however, resolved that their children would reap the opportunities open to them in America. Through scholarships and after-school jobs, Salk paid his way through the City College of New York, graduating in 1934. Though he debated whether to pursue a career in law or medicine, he finally chose medicine, and the next year entered medical school at New York University.

After Salk completed his internship at New York's Mount Sinai Hospital, he accepted a research position at the University of Michigan. With World War II coming to a close, scientists all over the world scrambled desperately to develop a vaccine to prevent a flu outbreak similar to the influenza pandemic that killed millions worldwide when the soldiers returned from World War I. At the University of Michigan, Salk sought to determine whether he could deprive the virus that causes influenza of its ability to make someone ill, and, at the same time, provide immunity to the flu. "We were told in one lecture," he once explained, "that it was possible to immunize against diphtheria and tetanus by the use of chemically treated toxins.... And the following lecture, we were told that for immunization against a virus disease, you have to experience the infection (in other words, chemical treatments wouldn't work).... What struck me was that both statements couldn't be true." When the young doctor pushed this point, no one could offer a satisfactory explanation. It didn't make sense. Salk's question stuck in his mind and provided the impetus to search for an influenza vaccine. His successful research lay the foundation for his approach to polio.

In 1947, Salk moved to the University of Pittsburgh School of Medicine, where he worked to develop a polio vaccine. He soon became the laboratory director. President Franklin Delano Roosevelt's battle with the disease had focused national attention on polio, and one of the president's associates started the March of Dimes, which raised money by publicizing sympathetic images of small children in wheelchairs and braces. Dr. Salk worked doggedly to produce an effective vaccine that would make such pictures disappear.

In 1952, polio struck more people than ever: 58,000 cases were reported, and 3,000 people died. The next year, after eight years of dedicated work, Salk announced that he had developed an experimental vaccine using a dead polio virus. The idea of injecting a polio virus, even a dead one, into a living person alarmed the public so much, Salk eased their fears by administering the vaccine to himself and his family first. In 1954, more than 1.8 million schoolchildren became "Polio Pioneers," participating in a nationwide test of the vaccine. It was history's largest medical experiment, and, miraculously, it worked. In 1955, the vaccine was pronounced "safe, potent and effective," and The Crippler's reign of terror came to a halt. By 1963, fewer than 1,000 cases were reported nationwide. Dr. Jonas Salk had saved the country's children.

Overnight, his name and face appeared on the covers of newspapers and national magazines. Some of his colleagues reacted jealously, but Salk carefully shared the credit for studying and preventing the disease. He even refused to patent his invention; it was more important to him that the medicine be distributed as widely as possible than that it yield a personal profit. In fact, he even felt uncomfortable when people called it the "Salk" vaccine.

During the 1970s and 1980s, Salk began to publish his thoughts on more philosophical matters. He set as his new objective "finding a cure for the cancer of the world": war. He traveled the globe delivering lectures on the possibility (and importance) of peace.

When the world of medicine called again, Salk did not turn his back. In the 1980s, AIDS reached horrifically epidemic proportions, and Dr. Salk, then in his seventies, came out of retirement to tackle this new killer. He co-founded a biotechnology company and devoted himself to developing a vaccine for AIDS. While engaged in this new project, he died on June 23, 1995, at the age of eighty.

At the time of Salk's death, California Governor Pete Wilson proclaimed, "His work not only saved the lives of children all over the world, but helped inspire generations of researchers that will one day put an end to the diseases of our day." Jonas Salk never stopped trying to help make the world a better place for all of us. He spent a lifetime seeking to solve problems that have beset the human race: influenza, polio, war, and AIDS. As he once said, "You can fail only if you stop too soon."

🍀 HISTORICAL IMPACT

The name Winston Churchill usually conjures up the image of a determined bulldog, both in demeanor and spirit. It's hard to imagine that as a youngster he was a wild, wayward, red-haired troublemaker. One of his school mistresses even described him as "the naughtiest small boy in the world!" His father, the leader of a prominent political group, feared that his young son would never qualify for a respectable profession. One day, when he saw young Winston playing with toy soldiers, he asked the boy, "Would you like to go into the Army?" That idea captured Winston's imagination and became the first great goal in his life.

Unfortunately, young Winston did not show much promise as a student, as his willfulness and impatience kept him from settling down to any regular course of study. He entered into the army class at Harrow, but failed—twice. Finally, a coach recognized some hidden spark in Churchill, gave the boy a low passing grade and allowed him to proceed to the military academy at Sandhurst.

Finally beginning to mature, or perhaps bolstered by the coach's confidence in him, Winston Churchill's academic career suddenly took a turn for the better. He soared to the top of his class, and found several new areas of interest, among them politics and literature.

Upon graduation, Churchill was assigned to the cavalry, where, far from any battlefield, he encountered a life of relative luxury and ease. The cavalrymen devoted much of their time to horsemanship, cricket and drinking games—activities that Churchill considered frivolous. A new seriousness had come upon this once unruly lad.

Churchill set two goals for himself: to fight and to write. The only opportunity to engage in the former was the war between Spain and insurgents in Cuba, so during his

Army leave, he convinced a London newspaper, the *Daily Graphic*, to pay him £5 to serve as a war correspondent. This meager sum would just offset the traveling expenses so he could go and join the fighting.

In 1896, Churchill's regiment traveled to India, where he spent his leisure time studying English literature, history, philosophy and science. When a minor skirmish broke out on the Northwest Frontier, he spent his leave, once again, acting as a war correspondent, this time for the *Daily Telegraph* and the *Allabahad Pioneer*. Throughout much of his early Army career, the young soldier continued this pattern: when not on assignment or fighting for the Army, he sought out fighting or writing elsewhere.

After Churchill resigned his Army commission in 1899, he was sent to cover the South African War for the *Morning Post*. He wrote descriptive and moving stories of his own capture, imprisonment, and escape from the Boers, accounts that raised him to the forefront of English journalists.

In 1900, Winston Churchill won his first election to public office as a Conservative parliamentary representative; soon, however, having angered his party with his outspoken and unorthodox views, he switched to the Liberal party. Politics, it turned out, satisfied his yearnings for a good fight and the eloquent expression of ideas. He served the British people in several different capacities, among them undersecretary for the colonies in the cabinet of Sir Henry Campbell-Bannerman, and president for two years of the Board of Trade. For a year after that, he acted as home secretary, where he fought for innovative labor reform and pension acts. In 1911, Churchill became first lord of the admiralty, presiding over the British naval expansion that preceded World War I.

Throughout that war and up until 1929, Churchill played some role in British politics. However, between

1929 and 1939, when the British government underwent a massive upheaval, Churchill could not gain any office in the new government. Still, he remained in the public eye through his writing. He also issued numerous warnings about the potential threat to Europe posed by the developing situation in Nazi Germany. No one heeded these farsighted admonitions.

When World War II broke out in September of 1939, the British Prime Minister, Neville Chamberlain, once again appointed Churchill first lord of the admiralty. Chamberlain himself proved a nerveless and ineffective leader, keeping his country on the sidelines when Nazi forces occupied Denmark and Norway in April 1940. In May, when the Germans invaded Holland and Belgium, Chamberlain could not bring himself to take decisive action and, after a great deal of public outcry, he resigned. That opened the door for Winston Churchill to become prime minister.

Upon taking office, Churchill warned the British people that he could offer them nothing more than "blood, toil, tears, and sweat!" When France seemed destined to fall to the Nazis, however, Churchill demonstrated his true mettle as a leader. Whereas Chamberlain had remained indecisive, Churchill acted with bulldog determination, declaring that Britain would fight against Nazi tyranny, even if it stood alone: "We shall fight in France, we shall fight on the seas and oceans, we shall fight with growing confidence and growing strength in the air. We shall fight on the beaches, we shall fight on the landing grounds, we shall fight in the fields and in the streets, we shall fight in the hills, we shall never surrender!"

Churchill's unwavering determination inspired the entire nation, rallying people to the cause of freedom. When Hitler sent his air force, the Luftwaffe, to subdue Britain before invading it, the slender British air force managed to fend them off. Men streamed from the towns hit by the Luftwaffe, volunteering to serve to the death in the Home Guard. The fortitude displayed by the British people forced Hitler to postpone the planned invasion and ultimately, to abandon it altogether.

In addition to inspiring his own countrymen to not give up the fight, Churchill also forged a bond of support with the United States and encouraged America to become involved in the war to save Europe. With President Roosevelt he hammered out an agreement on the Atlantic Charter, which pledged those who signed it to resist aggression, build a system of international security, and promote freedom, independence, and social progress throughout the world. After this agreement, the United States sped supplies to Britain to help turn the tide of the war.

Churchill became the ambassador for all those in the throes of the war resisting Nazi aggression. He traveled constantly, back and forth across the ocean—addressing the Congress of the United States and the Canadian Parliament, and visiting Moscow, Persia and Egypt, key battlefronts, and many international conferences. When World War II finally ended, on May 8, 1944, Churchill's perseverance paid off. He never, never, never gave up, and by doing so he made things go right for his own country and the entire world.

♣ PERSEVERANCE AND THE NEW MURPHY'S LAW

Truly successful people combat the three Fs with the three Ps, overcoming frustration, fatigue and failure with perseverance, patience and professionalism. Perseverance keeps you on the right path even when major obstacles cause frustration; patience keeps your eye on your ultimate destination even when tiredness sets in along the way, and professionalism—the constant refinement of your talent and skills—turns every failure into a new opportunity to realize your dreams.

In this chapter, we have encountered people who never gave up, no matter what frustration, fatigue or sense of failure they may have felt when the going got tough. They offer us five important lessons:

♣ **Lesson 1: Make Your Own Luck.** Matt Damon and Ben Affleck didn't sit around waiting for fortune to smile on them; they made their own luck by sticking to their guns, certain that they had the talent to succeed in Hollywood. Do you too often find yourself bemoaning your "bad luck"? When things don't go your way, do you sit and wait for someone else to make them go right, or do you take charge of the situation and work to create your own good luck? Good luck doesn't just happen to the lucky—it happens to those who act with determination. Use the three Ps to make luck happen for you.

♣ **Lesson 2: Strike the Word "Impossible" from Your Vocabulary.** Rudy Ruettiger did not give up when everyone told him he'd never realize his impossible dream. Do you ever let the pessimism of others deflate your optimism? Can you, like Rudy, weather the occasional chuckle or look of disbelief when you disclose your dream? Has an initial failure to accomplish a dream sent you home with your tail between your legs, or have you redefined that failure as an opportunity? There are no impossible dreams—only people who set their sights too low. Do everything possible to keep your sights set on your own "impossible" dream.

♣ **Lesson 3: Respond to Rejection with Renewed Resolve.** Beatrix Potter collected dozens of rejections for *The Tale of Peter Rabbit*, but she never let those rejections dispirit her. Does rejection depress you, or does it prompt you to strive even harder toward your goals? Have you ever countered a failure with a creative plan for success? Most great artists, writers and inventors suffered rejection before they finally achieved success. Rejection is not a stone wall, it's a stepping stone. When the going gets tough—get tough and keep going.

♣ **Lesson 4: Keep Setting Higher Goals.** Jonas Salk achieved many of the goals he set for himself, but after each victory, he set his sights on yet another one. Does successfully reaching a goal make you feel self-satisfied? Have you ever achieved a goal then sat back to bask in your success—or do you use one success as a springboard to even greater successes? Never forget that life is an unending journey and that a life well-lived requires one greater success after another.

♣ **Lesson 5: Grow Into Your Future.** Winston Churchill became an intellectual statesman and writer after an unpromising start. Do you ever feel impatient to achieve your goals, or do you realize that it usually takes time to grow into your future? Can you look back and see that you have developed your talent and skill in a way that will better enable you to attain your goals? Resolve to get better and better as you patiently persevere toward your dreams and develop the professionalism needed to realize them.

Patience. Perseverance. Professionalism. They provide the most effective antidotes to frustration, fatigue and failure. Remember this, if you remember nothing else: your dreams *can* come true—if you never give up.

Epílogue

♣ Pollyanna Was a Pessimist

A while back I found myself in a crowded conference room with two dozen healthcare executives. We had been discussing the problem of streamlining health-care delivery while at the same time improving the quality of service. After a couple of hours of heated debate about this seemingly unsolvable paradox, one weary hospital administrator sighed and muttered, "It's Murphy's Law. If anything can possibly go wrong, it will." As murmurs of agreement rustled throughout the room, a bright female voice exclaimed, "Murphy was an optimist!"

Everyone laughed, and that eased the tension long enough for me to start talking about the New Murphy's Law, that if anything should go right, the people assembled here—the most capable and energetic in their profession—could *make* it go right. A few minutes into my speech, I once again heard that bright female voice pipe up, "You're not a Murphy, you're a

Pollyanna." I couldn't help myself. Without skipping a beat, I shot back, "Pollyanna was a pessimist."

Again, everyone laughed, but the fellow who had first muttered about Murphy's Law—the *Old* Murphy's Law—waved his hand and asked, "I'd like you to explain that, Emmett." I did, and I'd like to conclude this book with how I responded to that request.

The original Pollyanna was the heroine of a novel by Eleanor Porter published in 1913. Her name has become a generic term, often used disparagingly, for someone who remains optimistic when more sensible people have resigned themselves to the consequences of an uncontrollably bad situation. While it's true that Pollyanna dealt with every situation, no matter how calamitous, with unbridled optimism, she also managed to find the good in everything. I called her a pessimist that day partly in jest, but partly to make this point: even if you remain irrepressibly optimistic, always looking for the good in everything, you will not *make* things go right unless you act on your optimism. Optimism without action adds up to no more than a wheelbarrow full of burnt oyster shells (to paraphrase H.L. Mencken).

Action. The ten rules in this book represent positive action you can take to make things go right. Although I have tried to arrange them in some sensible order, beginning with courage and concluding with perseverance, you can consider and practice them in any sequence because they do not form a step-by-step program as much as they do an *approach* to work and life, a way, as St. James admonished, to translate faith into action.

It's a little like golf, a game I play less than I watch, I must admit. A Tiger Woods or Ben Hogan brings much more to the game than a silky swing and a smooth putting stroke. They stride onto the course with a fierce determination to win within a strict framework of rules. For them, a golf game is more than the sum of its rules or the set of skills it takes to perform well; it is a synergy of all those things, and more. To win the Masters you need to do it all: strike the ball soundly, keep it on the fairway, chip it to the green, and roll it into the cup, hole after hole after hole, with patience, perseverance and professionalism every step of the way.

The same holds true for the New Murphy's Law. Winning the game of life and work takes more than the sum of the rules you've watched some fifty-plus people follow in this book. Practiced together with pragmatic optimism and strategic humility, they create a certain synergy: courage, connection, flexibility, empowerment, humility, time management, anger control, morality, generosity, and perseverance feed each other and feed off each other in a miraculous way, enabling you to reach higher, perform better and make anything that should go right, go more right than you ever dreamed possible.

I hope this page marks not the end of your quest to make things go right, but a new beginning—an opportunity to apply *The New Murphy's Law* to transforming the challenges of daily life into opportunities to feel "fantastic"—so that when you reach the end of your own days you can look back with few regrets and count all the ways you made things go right.

Thanks for joining me on this journey, and for the opportunity to share our Murphy family legacy.

Index

♣ B

♣ C

♣ D

♣ E

♣ F

♣

♣ **Q**

♣ **R**